Poems At The End Of The Rainbow

A Treasure of Poems
With a Different Style.
They'll Make You Think,
Wonder and Smile.

By
Jim Seaman

Writers' Branding
1-877-608-6550
www.writersbranding.com
media@writersbranding.com

Table of Contents

DEDICATION

As a 5th and 6th grade elementary school teacher, I taught many different types of poetry to my students. It was usually difficult and challenging, but always rewarding. I dedicated my first book to my students and thanked them for their efforts in rising above their own expectations.

My first or second year of teaching I introduced writing poetry. I told the students to just put a poem on paper. It could rhyme or not rhyme. We had not yet had any lessons on writing poetry, but I just wanted to see what the kids would come up with.

Following is a poem by a 6th grade student titled "This Person Inside"

> This person inside with
> Many feelings, sometimes it's
> Sadness, sometimes it's madness.
> The sadness part never shows
> Therefore nobody knows.
> The madness part nobody will see,
> Because it's hidden inside of me.
> Oh how I longed to let my feelings be free, but
> Not before I find this person inside of me.

My reaction and emotions to this student's poem was beyond amazement. My first thought was WOW!! The quality was of a professional poet. It is rare when someone can write a poem about their inner most feelings with a beautiful rhyme and a story to tell. My next thought was this student experiencing any of her written feelings and needed counseling? I talked to her and was assured she was fine.

Several years later I added a new type of poetry called alliteration. This is a poem where most words in the poem start with the same letter. Following is a poem by an eleven year old titled "The Swimming Salmon"

The salmon scared the shy steal head
As he swam sacredly from the
Swimming shark that scattered the
Swimming fish into the shape of a square
That safely swam away
In the sparkling sunlight in the shining sea.

These are just two examples of what students could accomplish when challenged with new types of writing assignments. To witness their learning abilities and see accomplishments beyond their imagination is a teacher's dream.

I therefore, as I did in my first poetry book, dedicate "Poems at the End of the Rainbow" to my students who rose to the challenge, conquered their doubts and became proud poets. Thank you all for not giving up and believing in yourselves. I sincerely hope that your classroom efforts followed you into the real world where you have had successful and rewarding lives.

FORWARD

I wrote a book of poems
So readers could reflect
Some will nod and agree
While others will reject.

Guns, justice, freedom
Stories of the day.
Some so controversial
You don't know what to say.

After it was published
I still had poems in me.
So with pen and paper
I had a rhyming spree.

A second book was born
'Bout our crazy nation.
Global warming, immigration,
Education and frustration,
Bullying and cooperation,
Covid and vaccination,
Politics and legislation,
Insurrection, devastation,
Abortion vs. preservation,
Adam and Eve and creation,
Slavery and discrimination,
Complication, imagination,
Wit and humor and elation,
Answers, questions, communication

My poems will feed your soul,
You'll smile or contemplate.
I hope you all enjoy
Lyrics that stimulate.

If They Only Knew

A couple hundred years ago
Our Founding Fathers said,
"We will all be free."
So equality was spread.

But they really all were hypocrites.
They each had many slaves.
What about THEIR freedom?
Seemed like many rights were waived.

So our leaders were not honest,
They did not give to all.
Until one day Lincoln
Decided to take that call.

So our nation went to war,
Young men left their farms.
Brothers fighting brothers
As each side took up arms.

When slavery was allowed,
Our leaders took in stride.
And when the war was over
Six hundred thousand died.

I believe it's safe to say
That our Founding Fathers roles
Was nothing short of murder
For 600,000 souls.

If they did what was right
Rather than ignore.
Than Lincoln would have lived
And there'd be no civil war.

Seems Okay to Me

Socialism, what does it mean?
It's a very misunderstood word.
Many are scared to hear it.
But this fear is really absurd.

Yes we know it's government run,
But don't be terrified.
It benefits society
So let's hear the other side.

Our military and medicare,
Police and education
Are all forms of socialism
And public transportation.

Our National Parks and FBI
Libraries and foster care
There's also social security
The post office and welfare.

So when people hear that word
They shouldn't worry or be afraid.
The additional help we get
Is a necessary upgrade.

Extinction of Words

I picked up a book to read one day
Titled Webster's Dictionary.
As I was turning the pages,
I noticed missing vocabulary.

Patriotism and compromise
I couldn't find anywhere.
Leadership and civility
Were also missing from there.

Common sense and truth
And freedom were also gone.
Bipartisan and agree
Appeared to be withdrawn.

Democracy and teamwork
Were missing from the book.
I couldn't find them anywhere
No matter where I'd look.

Their meaning no longer relevant.
These words no longer used.
Webster took them out
"Cause they always were abused."

Some Words of Wisdom

I heard some words by David Hogg,
A survivor of Parkland school.
His eloquent words of wisdom
Gave each of us some fuel.

We're in a desperate time,
Books parents want to ban.
To prevent our students learning,
They've devised a stupid plan.

But we know that books won't kill
Yet they want to take away.
But guns that murder in our schools
It's okay to let them stay.

A Currency Do Over

I'm looking at my money
And the faces on the bill.
But when I think of what they've done,
It makes me rather ill.

Most have owned several slaves.
The blacks were never free.
Yet these men were honored
Does not make sense to me.

How 'bout we make a change.
To those who've shown bravery,
Accomplishments or heroes
And those without slavery.

How 'bout Barrick Obama?
Martin Luther King a must.
Rosa Parks and FDR
All should be discussed.

Maybe Walt Disney,
His contributions count.
Jackie Robinson or Gates.
Names continue to mount.

Maybe Thomas Edison
And Neil Armstrong too.
Harriet Tubman was a go,
But Trump said let's undo.

(continued)

Or maybe Desmond Doss
Our greatest hero in war.
Or Congressman John Lewis
Whose part of political lore.

Some real greats omitted
As I present my case.
So turn the presses on.
Let's change the money face.

Postscript:
On the seven current bills
Let us hear your own voices.
Think about your options,
Then make your new choices.

Let's Fix Our Jury System

When guilt is overwhelming
And the jury sets them free.
Our legal system's broken
I can't believe what I see.

When evidence is lacking
And innocent sent to jails.
Our jurisprudence system
Is completely off the rails.

The system says to have
A jury by our peers.
But can they really judge?
Or do we have too many fears.

Prejudice and hate
Education way too low.
Driven by emotions.
Are they capable to know?

History has the answer.
Many mistakes are made.
The guilty often freed
And innocent betrayed.

The answer is quite simple
To eliminate this fury.
Justice made more fair.
Let's have a professional jury.

Highly educated.
They'll all get fairly paid.
They will judge all the facts
And their verdict won't be swayed.

What's the Number?

How many have to die?
In a mass shooting spree
By automatic weapons
To hear our begging plea.

Is there a body count?
A number we must reach.
Is it forty, sixty, eighty?
Before a shooting peace.

Twenty eight at Sandy Hook
But not enough dead.
Thirty two, Virginia Tech.
The GOP just turned their head.

Gun laws lax, too easy to get.
Too many continue to die.
Fifty dead at the Pulse nightclub.
That number still not high.

Sixty one in Vegas dead.
Four hundred more were shot.
Again the GOP
Uttered the words, "So What"

There's got to be a number
To finally change the law
But so far we haven't got there.
What will be the last straw?

(continued)

What if at the Capitol
Two hundred leaders died.
Would the GOP take notice?
And would new laws be applied?

Is there any number
Where violence will get through?
If a family member dies,
Will they finally open their eyes?

Maybe Precedent No Longer Applies

When someone questions laws
And it winds up going to court.
The judges may uphold
Or decide to not support.

They often look at settled law,
But does it still apply?
As time goes by we change
So it may not qualify.

The judge must take in mind
How we have changed the norm.
Times are now so different
The law may need reform.

But it seems that all too often
They look at precedent.
But it's from a different era
It's time they should dissent.

The Confession

A man commits a murder
Then confesses to a priest.
Someone else arrested.
Unable to be released.

Because the Catholic Church
Has a Confessional Seal,
The priest must be silent,
No names can he reveal.

The evidence is strong
As he sits and waits in jail.
His attorney not convinced
As he's denied bail.

There's' little hope for him
Though he didn't commit the crime.
He has a wife and kids
And surely will serve time.

Because the sinner confessed
He will have to be protected.
Justice is denied
And innocence neglected.

Narrow the Gap

Some make minimum wage,
Not much of a life to gauge.

While others make millions more
Their life made easy, it will soar.

Then there's those with billions,
It might as well be zillions.

There is no way to spend it all.
Their shopping spree soon will stall.

Too much gap between the two
Too much excess revenue.

Maybe there needs to be a way
To reduce the gap so all can play.

It seems not fair to leave some out.
What's this crazy life about?
So why not end this money drought
And make a change for a better route.

Maybe after a billion made
Send some excess to the underpaid.

The billionaire will still be rich.
While others climb out from their ditch.

Some will scream socialism,
But my eyes see as optimism.

A Different Time
A Different Place

Have you ever wondered what life would be?
If you lived at a different time?
The depression or covered wagons
Or mafia member and crime.

Traveling on a slave ship
Or jousting on a horse.
Building ancient pyramids
Or attacked with brutal force.

Tornadoes, floods or quakes
Storming a beach in war.
Roaming the desert with God
Or the life of a matador.

A concentration camp
Or living as a slave.
Homeless on the street
Or calling home a cave.

A plane that's going down,
Fight at the Alamo.
Born as deaf or blind
Or inmate on death row.

So if your rent is raised
Or your clothes no longer fit.
Or you get a flat to work
Or you find another zit

Maybe in the scheme of life
As your heading down the track,
Your life could be much worse,
So accept a little flack.

The Devil Made Me Do It

Is the Devil really present?
Can he invade our soul?
Can he transform evil?
And then take over control.

I recognize the answer now
From watching T.V. news.
Let me tell you how I know
And my revealing clues.

You see we have two governors
Whose behavior could only be
That Satan himself grabbed their souls
And they were no longer free.

Florida's Ron Desantis,
His functioning mind has quit.
And Texan Greg Abbott,
His righteousness has split.

I don't think it very possible
That the human mind could be
So callous and unfair
Without this evil glee.

They'll make schools unsafe,
Put good parents in our jail.
Take away the right to learn
And the vote they will curtail.

(continued)

This un-American way
Only the Devil could sell.
It had to come from him
When he cast his wicked spell.

Postscript:
I'm sure this poem has offended many members of the
Republican Party, but if you put what America stands for—
Democracy, Freedom, and the Pursuit of Happiness, then
this poem must be somewhat accurate.

The Ethics in Winning
(This poem is based on facts and not personal opinion)

It happened during the Sixties
Lombardi rose to fame.
The coach of the Green Bay Packers
Changed the structure of the game.

"Win at all cost", he said
The ethics out the door
No matter what it takes
It's important that we score.

Unlike the Olympic Games
Where competing is their creed.
It's not about the win
This lesson we must heed.

Vince Lombardi's motto
Found its way to the GOP
The rules changed to ensure
A win for their nominee.

Gone the moral code,
They lie, deceive and cheat
Whatever it takes to win
To guarantee their seat.

We'll block whatever they want
McConnell was heard to say
No more playing fair
We'll make sure it's done our way.

They Deserve to Be Noticed

They're many good deeds done.
They happen every day.
But most go unnoticed
They're just not on display.

We only hear of crime.
We only hear of hate.
The news is always bad.
We need to elevate.

So let's promote the good.
Let's educate us all.
Champion our heroes
And those who have stood tall.

Years

The years appear slow at first
But time quickly passes by.
Things put off another day
Until too late to satisfy.

You missed your children's games
Too many hours worked.
Now they're grown up,
A parent's job you shirked.

Trips you've planned to take
Things you wanted to buy
The years passed too quick
Unable to gratify.

You think there's always time
You ignore what should be done
But when you're old and cranky
You wonder what happened to fun.

You Can't Have It Both Ways

We're having a cultural war
On pro life and pro choice
We listen to both sides
As we hear their words and voice.

We also hear both sides
About getting the vaccine.
Many still say "no".
And say not to intervene.

These folks will argue with their heart
Their body is their own.
"So don't tell me what to do"
Their decision cast in stone.

But what I don't understand
Is the same group will say
Women can't have a choice
When abortion is in play.

You cannot have both ways
Or you'll be a hypocrite
Since they are both opposite
So pick one and commit.

A Misunderstood Word

We hear the word colleague
By Dems and GOP.
It means that they are friends
Even though they don't agree

They mistreat and also lie
They argue and they fight
They refuse to even listen
And believe they're always right.

They never compromise
Sometimes they're not polite
They frequently ignore
And sometimes they'll incite.

They reach across the aisle
To try to get it done
But there's no cooperation
They argue, turn and run.

It's upsetting when I hear
This word is really wrong.
I don't know why they use it
'Cause they never get along.

Postscript:
Friends must offer comfort
Friends must laugh and smile.
Friends must be respectful
And go the extra mile.

What Happens When We Can't Agree

A hundred sixty years later
You'd think we'd learn from war.
Instead we're still killing each other
It's the same as it was before.

Six hundred thousand dead
To fight to abolish slavery.
It never should have been
For each side to show it's bravery.

Now it's twenty twenty one
Another six hundred thousand dead.
But instead from bullets and cannon balls
It came from a virus we dread.

Our country split in half again.
Each side took up a stand.
Do I wear a mask or keep it off?
We watched it get out of hand.

Why can't we get together?
We're much more smart and brave.
A million may have stayed alive
Instead of going to their grave.

If the Boy Scouts Motto is to Be Prepared, Why Can't We?

How could we not be more aware?
How could we not better prepare?
Some even refused not to share.
It's almost as if we did not care
That patients unable to get their air.
Please tell me why the cupboard was bare.

Sanitizer, we could not find.
Orders for masks were not assigned.
Breathing machines were denied.
Our planning ahead was undermined.
People dying, America whined.
Those in charge deaf and blind.

And as we got closer to control the spread,
Test kits were gone, couldn't get ahead.
More dying at home and hospital beds.
The experts spreading gloom and dread.
So unprepared that they misread.

Medical reserves we must store.
You'll never know when you'll need more.
It's something we cannot ignore
Especially knowing what came before.

Postscript:
Trillions of dollars for defense
Stored in case we need to dispence.
How is it possible to be so dense?
To prepare for any consequence,

To Be A Hero You Don't Have To............

You don't have to get the game winning hit
Or win the playoff game.
You don't have to save a life
Or be in the Hall of Fame.

You don't have to be a soldier in war
Or a cop drawing his gun.
Or a fireman saving a life,
Or the pilot on Air Force One.

But you can be a hero
When you give one sound advice
Or when you know you should forgive
Or it's time to sacrifice.

Or raising a child to succeed
Or giving a pet a home.
Paying one a compliment
Or writing your wife a poem.

Giving up your seat on the bus,
Make someone sad smile
Give the guy with the sign a buck
Or going the extra mile.

You will not get a medal
Receive a plaque or award,
But what you have accomplished
Will be your inner reward.

Two Words

Two words not often heard
But bring a magical meaning.
They can change our life,
Open doors,
Open hearts.
Create opportunities
Provide new journeys.
An entrance of happy
A doorway of joy,
Fun and smiles,
Laughter and friends.
A change of pace.
A change of space.
A reaction.
A movement.
An energy.
Never ignore these two words,
But welcome them home.
Grab the new good
Hold on tight
Enjoy the ride.
Your life is about to change.
So what are these words?
Simply put:
"New Beginnings"

The Tale of Bail to Stay Out of Jail Is Off the Rail

Whenever a judge grants bail,
It seems like there's a flaw.
It always favors the rich.
We need to change the law.

The rich have money to post.
The poor will go to jail.
The rich go home to play.
The poor go off the rail.

It really seems not fair
The rich will get the break
Should not come down to wealth
It seems a gross mistake.

The Jury

Just heard this fact on the news
20% believe this tip.
That when we get vaccines
They're planting a microchip.

That's tens of millions of us.
Who accept this crazy quote.
What if they're on a jury
And they cast the deciding vote.

Young and Fearless

I watch the Olympics on T. V.
But there's one event I can't wait to see.
Women's gymnastics mesmerize me.
Their grace, their skills should not be.

The moves combined, the mental grind
Excellence which boggles the mind.

They fly through the air without a care.
They train and prepare to perform with flair.

They show no fear, they persevere
And when they perform we all cheer.

Obstacles, setbacks, injuries and pain,
They fall, they slip, they miss their grip.
Sometimes sprains, sometimes strains,
But their routines never mundane.
Their talent, their courage, their moves insane.

They enter the stage as they call their name.
They strive for medals and Olympic fame.

You Can't Change the Law at 30,000 Feet

(This poem is being written in the first person as a
narrative as I wanted to make it more impactful. But
please note it did not happen to me.)

I bought my ticket to fly
With Covid still scarring me.
But I knew we'd all be masked
Which the law would guarantee.

I was undergoing chemo,
My life no longer brisk.
I'm eighty years old
So I'm at a greater risk.

The plane was in the air,
My comfort level right.
But then I heard the words
Which caused serious fright.

The pilot would exclaim.
"No more masks to wear,
A judge just changed the law."
So masks removed midair.

The masks should have stayed
Until all were off the plane.
There's a chance that I could die.
This action was insane.

Texting vs. Calling

Why do we choose to text?
Is it to exercise our finger?
Why not choose to call?
I'd rather hear the ringer.

You text a comment or question
And hold on for your reply.
They answer back and then they wait.
You answer and then standby.

I miss the conversation
Where there is no need to wait.
I'd rather have the words be fluid.
So you can elaborate.

I miss the inflections and voice.
I miss the emotions and tone.
I miss the laughter and sounds.
So why not call on the phone.

Do You Watch the T. V. Ad?

When I turn the T. V. on
There's so many ads I see.
Each one worse than the other.
They make me want to flee.

They spend a million bucks
To try and make us buy.
But they're all so bad and dumb
Why would anyone comply?

In fact we usually walk away
To get a bite to eat
Or feed the dog or take a pee
Or maybe send a tweet.

So instead of paying for the ad
I have some good advice.
Why not take the cash they'll save
And lower the merchandice.

Let's Not Inflate the Price Tag

When they propose a bill
Why do they always quote
The cost for ten years
Seems harder to get the vote.

The price for one year
Seems easier to pass,
The number so much lower
More votes you could amass.

Which sounds better to you?
Three and a half trillion
Or the smaller price tag
Of three hundred fifty billion.

Dilemma

He had no job, no place to live
So he applied for Section 8.
He filled out forms and qualified
Then looked for real estate.

He found the perfect place,
But when they did a check,
They found his income low
And his credit was a wreck.

But if he had a steady job
And his credit was okay,
He still wouldn't qualify,
Not poor enough they'd say.

So when Section 8 says yes,
But the apartment answers no.
What was he to do?
Where was he to go?

Where Are the Seatbelts

We always keep our children safe
Whatever their culture or their race.
We guard and protect while in their space.
At school, home and every place.

Except when on a school bus
They seem to get off track.
The seatbelts that we each wear
Is something buses lack.

In a ten year period of time
Over 1300 died.
When they get on their school bus.
It must be safe to ride.

The Plight of the Indians

Our ancestors and those that came before
Were thieves and killers and even much more.

They stormed their land as blood was spewed.
They killed their buffalo and took their food.

They desecrated their holy place
And marched them to another space.

But in movies and books Indians blamed.
When all they did was protect their claim.

The whites would lie, they were not fair.
They had no honor and did not care.

We should be ashamed and show remorse.
We should feel guilt they took that course.

No difference if Russia would attack,
Win the war and tell us to pack.

Voices

There's 300 million in the USA.
All so different, none the same way
What do I mean you may query
The answer will leave us without a theory.
As we get older, our words we enounce.
The voices different when we pronounce.
Some are deep and some are low.
Others gruff and others flow.
Some are hoarse and some are croaky.
Some are throaty and some are smoky.
Some are soft and some are loud.
Some unique and make one proud.
But how strange it is that we can claim
That no two voices are the same.

Let's Make This Fight Fair

The gangs, cartels and thugs
Use an AK-47
And when they're in a fight
Their targets go to heaven.

When cops are called and they engage
They draw their 38's.
And as the bullets fly
The situation gravitates.

Is this an even match?
The weapons don't compare.
Seems like David and Goliath.
They need to make it fair.

Chapter 2

Life
A double scoop of ice cream
or a slice of moldy cheese

Yes You Can

There is a journey to be the best.
At times it may seem like a test.
Stop and breathe and take a rest,
But always aim for the crest.

Believe you can, believe you will
Believe in you and get that thrill.
Never stop, don't stand still.
Always know you've got the skill.

Build self-esteem, know you're great.
Don't delay or you'll be late.
Just know you can, it is your fate.
Remember that you're first rate.

So don't step back when there's life hazing,
But always know that you're amazing.

The Knock
(Written at 4:00 a.m.)

One day life knocked on my door,
I said "Hello," I want to soar.

I want to be great, I want to be me.
I want to fly, I want to be free.

Help me to see, help me believe.
Help me to know, help me to grow.

A journey of dreams, help me to cope.
A path to conquer and widen my scope.

I know I can, I know I will,
"Cause meeting you gave me the thrill."

Postscript:
This is a poem about interpretation and conscientiousness.
When life knocked on my door, what is life? My inner self,
a blueprint for my life, God, an inner voice, my soul speaking.

What is the answer? The answer for me is there is no answer.
It is a metaphor for what you want your journey in life to be like.

It's A Different World Now

I believe in happy endings,
But it's hard to realize.
The obstacles and nightly news
Mean we have to fantasize.

What's happened to smiles and happy cheers?
Why so many frowns and tears?
Why has applause turned to jeers?
Why are we so cavalier?
Why does evil interfere?
Why is our life so full of fear?
Why do so many continue to sneer?
Why are so many insincere?
Why does happiness disappear?
Can joy and laughter reappear?
Can we once again persevere?

How You Know You're Getting Old

When you look at your hands and see those blots.
You wish they were measles and not age spots.

The lawns too big to mow and weed.
Your arms to short when you want to read.

It's harder to take a driving vacation.
You're now getting mail for cremation.

The gym's a dream, jogging no more.
Too many trips to the pharmacy store.

When your children turn fifty that's not a good sign.
And that crepe paper skin means you're now in decline.

Your days are shorter, in bed by ten.
You get up to pee again and again.

There is no need for a second car.
You're taking classes in CPR.

You need to get help to clean your house.
It's too much to handle for you and your spouse.

To change the channel you grab your phone.
And when you gain weight it's not muscle tone.

Yikes, at least I'm still alive
I think I'll celebrate and go sky dive.

Choosing the Right Unknown

Some things change, some stay the same.
Some a challenge, some are tame.
Some days I run, some days I walk.
Some days I'm quiet, some days I talk.
Some days I'm weak, some days I'm strong.
Some days I'm right, some days I'm wrong.
Some days I climb, some days I fall.
Some days I hide, some days I'm tall.

But every day, can be bright.
Just seek what's right and see the light,
To push aside all that's trite.
To grab the best with all your might.
To find what's special that's out of sight.

Throw away, all those sneers.
Rid yourself of ugly tears.
Vacate all unwanted fears.
And open your life to smiles and cheers.

Grab the Good

I think of the trials and smiles of life.
The turn styles we enter, the profiles we dial.
Some are short, some go for miles.
It can be fragile and sad or happy and glad.
It can turn as we learn, it can burn as we yearn.
The ups, the downs, laughter or frowns
Sometimes it's luck, sometimes we're stuck.
It's a mystery to find, it grinds at our mind.
It complicates and captivates,
It aggravates and motivates.
We laugh, we cry, we quit, we try.
Some will crash, some will fly
Some will live, some will die.
But we all received the gift of birth
To create our worth on this green earth.

What Happens When Arrogance Lifts It's Head

Teamwork's the engine to drive success.
While conceit and arrogance find distress.

Whether in business, sports or love,
Working together sets us above.

Showcasing unity is better than one.
Cooperation will always get things done.

When you go it alone it's not the same.
When you go without help you'll lose the game.

Teamwork's applied in most of our life.
To win the cause or go without strife.

When Covid invaded it changed us all.
It was urgent that each had to stand tall.

If we stood apart thousands would cry.
If we turned our back thousands would die.

But when experts said what we had to do
Too many replied, "No thank you."

Some were defiant and went their own way.
The results were death 'cause they wouldn't obey.

A Garden Planted With Love

The sun is out, spring is here,
My garden needs to grow.
I wanted to make it easy
So I grabbed my handy hoe.

The first container to plant
Was one they called trust.
I knew it would take some time
But eventually be robust.

Next I planted laughter
With a twinkle in my eye.
I knew that it would flourish
And smiles would magnify.

I found a spot for happiness
And dug a hole just right.
I hoped the buds would spread
To make our life more bright.

Next in the ground, compassion.
The others would feel better.
I would need to water often
To become a trendsetter.

I turned and grabbed another
This one full of joy.
Soon it would spread delight
That I would soon employ.

(continued)

The next one I would plant
Was one that we call fun.
To help it grow tall,
Would require lots of sun.

Another one to plant
So I dug the perfect hole.
Honesty went in the dirt
To soon improve our soul.

There's one more left to go
It's integrity by name.
If you watch it sprout and grow
It'll help to win the game.

The last thing I would need
As I put on my gardening glove.
Was to fertilize so it would grow
So I spread a bag of love.

Life on a Pogo Stick

Bad day at work or flunked a test.
Something you need to get off your chest.

Too many bills that are past due
Lost someone really close to you.

Car won't start, got a stomach ache.
Facing tremors from a quake.

Too much weight gain, clothes won't fit.
When you look in the mirror you see a zit.

You find your teen now on drugs.
You were attacked by a group of thugs.

What more is there that can go wrong?
You wonder how you will stay strong.

Don't sit still, but think it through
Take aim, take charge, know what to do.
Don't refuse the impromptu
Push yourself so you'll pursue.
Mix some "happy" in your brew.
Try a smile to change your view.
Treat yourself to something new.
Say a prayer, God loves you.
Call a friend to help your "blue".

Sometimes life goes off the track
Obstacles, sress or panic attack.
Grab this luggage, start to unpack,
Put things in order, you'll bounce right back.

Starting Over

Hit a bump, off the track.
Too many things that you still lack.
You can find your four leaf clover.
It's not too late to start over.
Don't look back, but move ahead
Fears and tears you will shed.
You're bright and stronger than you think,
So you will find your missing link.

Tired of Waiting

I'm tired of believing what America could be.
I'm weary of waiting for us to agree.
I'm drained while I wonder if compassion I'll see.
I'm worn out as I ponder if they'll hear our plea.
I'm puzzled as I ask if they'll find the key.
I'm confused as I question if hatred will flee.
Will we ever become a V.I.P.
I'm doubtful there'll be a productive spree.
Wouldn't it be great for a guarantee,
To one day rise to the Land of the Free.

What is the "It Factor"?
(It is when ....)

You captivate......they listen
You radiate.......they smile
You illuminate......the room
You elevate......their minds
You fascinate......they're interested
You navigate......they follow
You stimulate......they react
You cultivate......they improve
You exhilarate......they're happier
You advocate......they believe
You invigorate......they energize
You motivate......you move them
You appreciate......they're thankful
You inflate......their persona

I'm on Vacation

Let's head down the fun highway:
Monday I'll drive to the sandy bay.
Tuesday lunch at the new café.
Wednesday a movie at the matinee.
Thursday I'll see my first ballet.
Friday the telescope and Milky Way.
Saturday golf and even croquet.
Sunday I'll see a concert or play.

So stay away
From a gray day.
Don't delay
Or go halfway
Smile and play
It's the only way
To be happy and gay
So you should say,
I got it, okay!

Postscript:
So here's my challenge to each of you.
To write a poem that we can view.
Make it rhyme as you pursue.
Good luck with your new debut.

Make it fun like Irish stew
Or anyway that you can do.
But don't give up like Waterloo.

Chapter 3

Reflections
Take a moment

(continued)

Vaccine as a Metaphor
What Would Life Be Like…?
What About the Doctor's Oath?
It's Gotta Be a Dream
Why Should We Gamble With Human Lives?
A Billion Dead
Better Off Where I Am
Better Safe Than Sorry
Enough is Enough
Gun Violence by the Numbers
Time
Their Life Cut Short
All the Good We'll Never See

Waiting

Adam and Eve looked down one night
What they saw was sadness and a pitiful sight.

Centuries of greed and hatred toward man,
This was never part of the Father's plan.

Where was compassion they taught mankind?
It seems over time it got left behind.

What happened to peace and joy toward all?
It didn't take long for laughter to stall.

Their tears of sorrow are the droplets of rain.
The thunder their cries of despair and pain.

In horror, but hope, they watch each day,
To see if we ever will find our way.

Empty Hopes and Dreams

My name is Grace and I'm now dead
Shot at school in the back and head.

Ten others also died that day
When we became the shooter's prey.

Hopes and dreams I'll never see.
Goals and jobs will not be.

No marriage, kids, travel or pets,
But only sadness and regrets.

All stolen by the GOP
Their hopes and dreams they will see.

Gun laws to lax, but they don't care
Lives are taken, they won't repair.

I hope when they all sleep at night
They'll see my face then make it right.

The Sadness and Madness Are Back

The tears and fears appear to be here.
The sadness and madness return.
The shouts ring out and people fall.
The children bawl, the wounded crawl.
The innocent Asians are targets.
Others were slaughtered in markets.
Our leader incited and bypasses the masses.
His minions refuse to mend.
The Senate refuses to bend.
America's at wits end.
The crazies off track, they fire and attack.
The sadness and madness are back.

Our Republican minds won't change.
They laud their praise to the NRA.
On their way to the firing range.
Meanwhile the shooter raises his gun.
All you see is smoke and dead kin folk.
It quickly began, but after his run, his deed was
done.
The bullets flew in a sea of rage.
He's followed his script like he was on stage.
20,000 killed by guns each year.
The GOP sneers, they have no tears.
Their message sent and oh so clear.
Their hearts are lacking, their soul cracking.
No fix or change anywhere in sight.
They turn off the lights and say good night.
The flaws in the laws still remain.
More people die, the people cry.
The bullets will continue to fly.

March 3, 1991

He was beaten by cops for a DUI
He got on the ground and would comply.

But the cops decide to kick and taze.
His body jolted with electric rays.

Four cops attacked, twelve more would watch,
Their batons received another notch.

But the cops didn't know what lay ahead
As Rodney King screamed and bled.

It was caught on film for the world to see.
Rodney's plea and the beating spree.

They went to court and three were free,
Our rights no longer guaranteed.

After the verdict justice yearned
So the blacks rebelled and L. A. burned.

Rodney had some words to say
From that horrific and gruesome day.

His words of wisdom spoken strong
"Why can't we all get along?"

Six words that bring tears to my eyes
They electrify and unify
They amplify and magnify.

An anthem for all that we belong
"Why can't we all get along?"
"Why can't we all get along?"

How to Fix Us

They say our country is the best
Standing above all the rest.
But what I see, I'm not impressed.
It seems to me we failed the test.

Those words fall short I propose.
Laughter gone, no more rainbows.
Too much hate, too many woes.
The magic gone, we've decomposed.

No good in sight, it's getting worse.
We function like we're in reverse.
We're spiraling down as we transverse.
As if we're living under a curse.

What can we do to have success?
What can be done to stop this mess?
We need to end this distress.
The lies and anger must digress.

We need to embrace and rise above.
We need to remove the boxing glove.
We need to go from hawk to dove.
We need to change to show more love.

Did I Do Something Wrong?

Things not the same in the marriage game
There's no more flame, am I to blame?

Mom and Dad always fight.
It makes me sad, there's tears at night.

There's no more magic, no more caring,
I hear them swearing, I see them glaring.

Loving off course, they have no remorse.
They argue and yell, then talk of divorce.

I try to be strong, wished they got along
I ask myself did I do anything wrong?

At times it's scary, will mom remarry?
The uncertain times make me wary.

Will I be glad or maybe sad,
If one day enters a brand new dad?

Will he give advice, will he be nice?
Or no baseball games and cold as ice.

Some days there's tears, some days there's fears
Some days it's clear some days I veer.
Some days I'm able to persevere
Some days I want to disappear.

What I face is hard to embrace.
At times I wish I could erase.
When I go to sleep there's dreams I chase.
When I awake, it's a different pace.

(continued)

I never imagined through searching eyes
That family ties and lullabies
Would be replaced with lonely cries.

That's Not Possible

Trump said they bring in drugs
Hispanics rape and kill.
We have no use for them
They offer us no skill.

He spent billions for a wall
To keep Hispanics out.
He locked children up in cages
Send Dreamers home he'd shout.

What's hard for me to get
Is over thirty percent
Gave their vote to Trump
Where is there malcontent?

Bring Back Wyatt Earp

When I turned the T. V. on
I thought it was a joke.
It couldn't be this insane
I thought they had misspoke.

They said if you lived in Texas
You could now carry your gun.
No need to have a permit
It would apply to everyone.

Will it be like watching Gunsmoke?
Will they practice their quick draw?
Will guns be worn on your belt?
Is this a reasonable law?

Bring back Wyatt Earp
And the fight at the O K Corral
Just think of all the stories
That each of us could tell.

What about too many drinks
Arguments or road rage
Or those that are unstable
As they draw their guns to engage.

Is the Price to High?

Almost a trillion spent
To make our enemies fear.
In case we had to fight
We'd hope they would stay clear.

Planes, bombs and ships
Are all the very best.
We're a nation of power and strength
Far above the rest.

So what happened in Vietnam?
And then Afghanistan?
We failed to win the wars.
What happened to our plan?

Thirty years of battles,
Sixty thousand dead.
Countless lives ruined,
Three hundred thousand bled.

Maybe we're not that good.
The enemy's always strong.
Maybe the choice of war
Is unacceptable and wrong.

We need to ask ourselves
Should we get involved?
Maybe there's a better way
To get this thing resolved.

Lock Up Mom and Dad

Our country's in need of help
But somehow it got much worse.
It's as if we're playing a game.
And drew the card with the curse.

Idaho State just passed a law
Sending parents to jail forever.
For providing the right to medical care
For their trans kids life's endeavor.

And if that's not bad enough
If they go to another state,
They could still go to jail for life.
Is it possible to have such hate.

Does government have the right
To take away mom and dad.
All there doing is being a parent
To their child's own launching pad.

Knowing That You Can

Never forget who you are, raise that bar, you are a star.
Never forget the knowledge you own, so get in the zone,
you're not alone.
Never forget what went before, there's so much more, your life can soar.
Hold on with pride, enjoy the ride, increase your stride,
remain bright eyed.
You will achieve, plan to conceive, always believe as you perceive.

Where Are the Kevlar Vests?

We went to war in Iraq.
Our soldiers said goodbye.
But many lacking Kevlar vests
To wear so they wouldn't die.

Not enough to go around
The Army unprepared.
How could this have happened?
Their safety was impaired.

Family and friends stepped up.
Homemade vests were sent
Our soldiers scrounged through landfills.
A nation of malcontent.

"You go to war with what you have
And not with what you want."
These ugly words from Rumsfeld
Seemed rather nonchalant.

700 million spent each year.
That's planned for our defense.
So where's the Kevlar vests?
What a terrible consequence.

It's So Bazaar, I Can't Even Think of a Title

Friday and Saturday night
They'll head to the local bar.
They'll dance, drink and party
Unable to drive their car.

Somehow they'll find their house
Barely able to walk.
Drowsy lacking judgement
Barely able to talk.

They might be falling down
Seizing and poor vision.
Headaches even a coma
And lacking in precision.

Puking all night long
Not much to dignify,
Waking up in pain
It's possible they could die.

Friday night rolls back again
They'll head right back for more.
They'll dance, drink and party
Consequences they'll ignore.

I Don't Get It

December 7th '41
Is a day we won't forget.
But how did we let this happen?
Unaware of the coming threat.

19 ships crippled or lost
Over 3000 killed or hurt.
Hundreds of planes taken out.
Where was the warning alert?

Few may know the truth
That Japan was on their way.
But we had broken their code
And knew about that day.

We knew the bombs were coming
We knew their ships were near.
So why weren't we prepared?
The answer is unclear.

Looking Back

I don't want to live my life
That when I look back.
There's things I never did
And memories that I'll lack

Trips I only dreamed.
Asking someone out.
Friends I never called
Or having too much doubt.

Dining out more often
Things I never bought.
Being more spontaneous.
A class I could have taught

Leagues I never joined.
I thought about a cruise.
Running a marathon
Or visiting local zoos.

Hobbies I'd have liked
Getting on a game show.
Competing in a contest.
Or helping in skid row.

Coaching Little League,
Signing up to take a class.
Learing how to dance
Or making stained glass.

(continued)

Learning to play an instrument
A garden in your yard.
Trying for better grades
Tearing up your credit card.

Change your hair or grow a beard
Take time to volunteer.
Get a pet or two.
Change a boring career.

So don't procrastinate
Push yourself so you'll pursue.
Don't forget the memories,
You have to follow through.

As time passes by
And you think it is too late.
But don't give in to time
Just open up your gate.

My First House

Prices go up as time goes by.
Things that were cheap are now sky high
My first house that I would buy
Was a fair price, I could justify.

Inflation hit and less could achieve.
No one could predict, no one could perceive.
What a car now cost, I can't conceive.
More than my house, it's hard to believe.

My Expired License Tags

I'm driving in my car
When the blinking lights appear.
I pull my car to the curb
With nothing I should fear.

Two officers get out
And slowly walk to me.
I have no dread or panic
As they ask for my I. D.

"Your license tags expired,"
They said to me that morning.
"Instead of giving a ticket,
I'll let you off with a warning."

No worries or concerns
The cops were very polite.
No search or lights in my face,
Because my skin was white.

Our Forefathers Tears

Asians being blamed for covid.
Blacks being targets and die.
Our leaders claim we're the best
As their ignorance becomes their lie.

Immigrants mistreated and jailed.
Their children are taken away.
They're housed behind barbed wire.
Our leaders say this is okay.

The Jews and other religions
Are attacked and murdered as well
What's wrong with our nation you ask?
It's as if we are under a spell.

Prejudice, bullying, sedition
Are part of the American way.
Our leaders do nothing to stop
As America slips away.

Please Hear My Silent Screams

I need a new pair of shoes.
My only ones hurt my feet.
But I make the minimum wage
So my shoes are a distant treat.

I'd love to have a steak,
But this meal is only a dream.
Because I make the minimum wage
All I hear is my silent scream.

My car is in the driveway,
I travel with a bus pass.
But I make the minimum wage
So I cannot afford the gas.

My clothes are from Goodwill,
I would love to take a trip.
But I make the minimum wage,
So it's hard to get a grip.

The Dems have tried to change,
'But it's been longer than twelve years.
What a horrible life to live.
The wisdom seems quite clear.

How am I supposed to live
On seven twenty-five an hour?
But Republicans don't seem to care
As they have all the power.

How 'bout we switch our pay
And they'll make the minimum wage.
How fast do you think it'd take
To eliminate this outrage?

Penny's and Nickels

To make a penny cost two cents
So why do we bother to mint?
It's a loss that we all pay
Let's change this coin blueprint.

The cost of a nickel to mint
Is also a loss we pay.
It cost eight cents to make.
Shouldn't there be a better way?

Remorse

(While this poem may seem difficult to read,
it is brutally honest and presents a powerful message.
My goal in writing this was to protect and save the
live's of children)

Parents say no to masking their kid.
Their parenting skills are off the grid.

Kid gets virus, enters ER.
Recovery comes with such a high bar.

The kid gets worse and eventually dies
The parent's grief magnifies.

Mom and Dad miss their kid,
Because of the mask that they forbid.

I watch T.V. and see a crowd.
I hear them shout clear and loud.

"No More Masks" is what I hear.
The lack of logic, cavalier.

Thousands more will surely die
As they continue their battle cry.

Mom and Dad cannot believe
As they continue to cry and grieve,.

Postscript:
They're way too young to choose their fate.
They need their parents to illuminate.
And when they don't, the children pay
"Cause Mom and Dad didn't know the way."

So Many Choices

I go to the box to pick up the mail
Some bills, some junk, some turn me pale.

Donations they seek for those in need.
They're all important as I hear them plead.

Environment, pets, G. I.'s and more,
Cancer, and heart, they're hard to ignore.

Children and those in need of food,
It's hard to decide which ones to include.

Wildlife, Shriners, St. Jude and bees,
Elephants, Peta and refugees

Docs Without Borders and my candidate
Police who have died, I now hesitate.

I want to help, I know I must,
But funds are low so I try to adjust.

My choices many, they're neck and neck,
I finally decide and mail a check.

I rotate monthly and send two more.
I feel good, my spirits soar.

Stolen Lives

This poem has taken sixty years to write.
I had to live it to get it right.

Heartaches, heartbreaks, nightmares, despair,
Generations of suffering, life not fair.
A life impaired, no one cared.
Glares and stares and prayers unanswered

Many declare they're not the same
Not equal to us, not in the game.

The history books made it real
The T.V. news made me feel,
But no matter what, we could not heel
Their dignity, some would steal.

Too many died by cops and Klan
A noose and tree, a short lifespan.

A life we stoled, a life we wrecked
No respect, but only neglect.
What we need is an architect
To plan the healing and correct.

Let's set them free a second time.
Let's rectify this horrible crime.

The Best of My Me

I always give the best of me
The best I can do, the best I can be.

Whether at school or work or play,
It's something for us to do every day.

Never half-way, lazy or slack,
Always move forward, never look back.

If you need help, there's others to ask.
Whatever the deed, whatever the task.

Follow this course and then you will shine.
Aim high to cross the goal line.

An Agonizing Choice

Sometimes we have to make
A choice that is not easy.
We wonder, think and cringe
Our actions make us queasy.

What if you could drop a bomb
To end a world war.
But 200,000 innocent
Would die and be no more.

A horrible choice to make
But if you were under the gun
Just ask President Truman.
What would you have done?

The Arrival of Ghost Guns

My name is Joe, I'm only ten.
I got in a fight at school.
He was a kid I did not like,
He made me look like a fool.

I knew what I had to do
So I devised a plan.
Had to be brave and bold
Stand up and be a man.

I went online to search
Where I found a ghost gun.
There was no number on it
Any age could purchase one.

No paperwork to file.
No background check to get.
You have to assemble the gun.
There's help so do not fret.

A felon or mentally ill,
A kid whose underage,
Serial killer or rapist
Or anyone with rage.

These are ones who can buy
Sent by postal mail.
It skirts around the law.
The killers now prevail.

The Legacy of the GOP

They'll change the rules and make new laws
Whatever it takes to promote their cause.
They control the vote so they will win.
No more ethics, but rather a sin.

I think back to war when G.I.'s died,
Family cried, America sighed.
Lost limbs and stares and wheelchairs
Only despair and chilling nightmares.

Their cause was freedom and to guarantee
Our democracy and we stay free.

But just around the corner I fear
These rights will turn and disappear.
The right to elect no longer here.
Our nation's path no longer clear.

Did our G. I.'s suffer and die in vain
Will we no longer, thrive and gain.
Are we watching freedom go down the drain.
What an awful legacy and nasty stain.

The Shopping Cart
(A True Story)

Everything he owned
Was in his shopping cart.
I sensed his hidden tears
Streaming from his heart.

He slowly walked alone
And crossed the lonely street.
A sleeping bag and tattered clothes
And tired swollen feet.

Darkness in his life
Shelter he would seek.
I watched him push ahead
As tears rolled down my cheek.

Postscript:
What's wrong with this I ask?
How can this be?
We must open up our eyes
To mend their silent plea.

They Need To Be Recognized

Veterans have their day
Our labor gets one too.
And on the 4th we celebrate
The red, white and blue.

We honor the birth of Christ
Presidents get their day.
On Easter we hide eggs.
The kids are happy and gay.

We celebrate Moms and Dads
Thanksgiving we all share.
And then on Cupid's Day,
Love is in the air.

We honor those who gave their life.
Columbus has his day.
And recently we added one
To honor MLK.

But there's a special day we lack.
We need to add one more.
They're brave in what they do.
They make our spirits soar.

They care and hold our hands.
They care and give us hope.
Some will even die.
They're fearless and help us cope.

(continued)

When Covid struck us down,
Docs and nurses were there.
Paramedics and other staff
Sacrificed their own care.

They need our gratitude.
We need to recognize.
We need to tell them thanks
With a very special prize.

We must dedicate a day
The World celebrates.
We must show them that we care
As our love illuminates.

To Macho To Learn

When the AIDS epidemic attacked
We all came off the track.

We preached safe sex and hoped for the best,
But far too many failed the test.

No condoms, no testing, no common sense.
Too many faced the consequence.

As a result 30 million dead,
No country safe, it invaded and spread.

Forty years later and covid is here.
You'd think we had learned from all that fear.

Six feet away and wear a mask.
A simple request the docs would ask.

But too many said no, and went their own way,
Refused the vaccine and would not obey.

They thought they were safe, to macho to care.
Their bodies struck down, too late for a prayer.

Too many said they wouldn't comply.
Too many said they won't unify.
Too many said they will defy.
Too many didn't listen and they would die.

What's wrong with us, why didn't we learn?
Why did so many take the wrong turn?

(continued)

Postscript:
But the 7 million who died
Took the innocent to their grave.
Kids and teachers, nurses and docs.
The same as a terriorist wave.

Vaccine as a Metaphor

The Covid snuck into our lives.
It did not spare us, but rather dared us.
It chased and embraced as we tried to trace.
Thousands died as we tried to erase.
The scientists would intervene
And soon we had a new vaccine.

But our task has only just begun
There's much more work that needs to be done.
There's another virus that stirs among us.
So let's fix the surge of hate
We can no longer wait to eradicate.
So let's end the game and call checkmate.

And about the challenge of drugs
There are no hugs, but only shrugs.
As the deaths continue to grow
We need a syringe of hope.
We need to be able to cope.
We need to get off this tightrope.
And destroy the status quo.

So let's get back to the lab.
It's time that poverty ends.
We need to ascend
And no longer pretend
We must have a living wage.
As it spreads across America
Let's attack with fierce rage.

(continued)

Politics is sick
And desperately in need of a cure.
Our leaders continue to be immature,
Our leaders continue to remain impure.
We need to insure we take a detour
To fix this ugly pandemic.
We despise the lies,
America cries,
We urgently need to revitalize.

Education is in the toilet
Learning like Russian roulette.
Low scores continue to spread.
We've got to get outa bed.
We must strive to get ahead
We have the tools to vaccinate
We must return to be first rate.

Voting rights are getting hard.
Each year we have new strains.
Equality getting jarred
We have to make more gains.
How 'bout a shot in the arm
That will take away the harm.

Too easy to get a gun.
The crazies keep on killing.
Too much blood is spilling,
We need to stop, God willing.
Children die in schools
We need to change the rules.
This epidemic needs to end.
What if it was your child?
I bet then you'd comprehend.

(continued)

Black Lives Must Matter to each and all
We need to stop this free fall.
This wrong must have a cure
We no longer can endure.
It seems the cops don't learn
We need to yearn to see it turn
Equality must be pure.

Society rests on life support.
Our actions continue to always fall short.
We need to arrange to find cures that change
We've conquered our problems before
So now it's time to change the score.

What Would Life Be Like............?

What would life be like
Without cell phones or T. V?
Video games and Amazon
Or drinks that're sugar free?

Facebook, twitter, blogs
Netflix and computers
Trips to the covered mall
And GPS and ubers.

Lattes, google, Costco
Power mowers for the yard.
Home and fire alarms
And a Visa credit card.

Selt belts and the gym
Wendy's and Dairy Queen
Vegas, Tablets, kindles
And the giant T.V. screen

Cars, planes and pizza
Air conditioning and a cruise
Washers, dryers, stoves
Vaccines and barbecues.

How could we have coped
How could we have fared
I guess we'll never know
'Cause we'd be unaware.

What About the Doctor's Oath?

There are too many doctors
Who refuse to treat your pain.
The patient needs relief,
But the doctor will refrain.

They're afraid you will abuse.
They're afraid that you will crave.
They're afraid you won't get off.
Some even fear your grave.

"But what about my pain?
Nothing else will help me cope.
What am I to do?
This is my only hope."

"I can't get out of bed
I cannot sleep at night.
I can barely get around.
Please help me with this fight."

"I plead to get relief.
I promise I will follow
The directions on the bottle.
Just give me the pill to swallow."

"There is no record of abuse.
There's nothing in my chart.
But the doctor still says no
Refusing to do his part."

The doctor must use judgement
To consider risks and pain.
But isn't it malpractice
When they take their oath in vain?

It's Gotta Be A Dream

My life's been pretty full
Decades to be exact.
So many things have happened
Not much that it has lacked.

It's like watching a day soap opera
Or a streaming T. V. show.
You never know what's next
Peace or another blow.

Murder, mayhem, misery,
It's got to be a dream.
Life cannot be this bad.
We're running out of steam.

Bombs at a marathon,
Cops shoot you in the back.
Death at a peaceful march
It's harmony we lack.

Emergence of more hate groups.
Our Capitol attacked.
The guilty have gone free,
Our freedoms have been sacked.

Then we've got politics.
They lie and then they cheat.
There's no more hope or honor
Trust replaced by deceit.

I must be dreaming this.
No way it can be true.
No compassion or goodwill.
It's like living in a zoo.

Why Should We Gamble
With Human Lives

There's one thing that I fail to grasp
When I question I only gasp.

I shudder, I quiver and wonder
I don't understand their blunder.

Why do so many doubt?
The result could be human drought.

Global Warming won't take a break.
Our planet has too much at stake

Let's listen to what experts say.
So let's act now and not delay.

They've given us something we all hear.
The consequences we need to fear.

It would be foolish to roll the dice
And then ignore the proven advice.

We all want children to be alive.
Why gamble to see if they'll survive.

We need to believe and do our part
So now's the time we need to start.

A Billion Dead
(And for What?)

With the horrors of war it's hard to keep score
As the death toll soars each nation abhors.

Peace talks fail, destruction prevails,
The babies wail as the bombs derail.

The battle cries roar, what a dreadful eye soar
You ask what it's for, it enters our core.

Sometimes for land, they want to expand
Sometimes for greed when they feel the need.
The people plead and then they bleed.

Sometimes for power to show their might.
Sometimes to show that they are right.
Sometimes they just want to incite.

The final tally when all is said,
A billion dead, while millions fled.
The atrocity of coffins and real bloodshed.

Better Off Where I Am

Surroundings new and still a blur
My name I still don't know.
You see I'm still in mom
Haven't yet to say hello.

As I wait to travel out
I hear the lies and hate.
Where's kindness and goodwill?
Confused while I still wait.

So peaceful where I am
With compassion, love and bliss.
I don't like what I hear
Why does life become like this?

I'll soon be part of that,
My time inside not long.
Where's the peace and laughter?
This mood and gloom so wrong.

I contemplate my future.
I reflect about my life.
I think I'd rather stay inside
Than be part of so much strife.

Better Safe Than Sorry

Global warming's here.
Can't dispute that it's severe.
It's all over the hemisphere
And something we should fear.

So why do many sneer.
They think it's nowhere near.
As they deny and jeer.
Do they think it will disappear?

Their attitude's unclear
As they laugh and have a beer.
But it's getting worse each year.
So why so cavalier?

Enough is Enough

"We Shall Overcome"
Is a 'Civil Rights Song'
It gave the blacks hope,
But it's been way too long.

Centuries of endless suffering,
Decades of grief and pain,
Progress way to slow
As they traveled down that lane.

Lynching's while they wait.
Burnings while on pause.
Hatred every day.
What's happened to this cause?

Gun Violence by the Numbers

8 children die from guns.
This happens every day.
32 more wounded,
The guns not locked away.

50 years of carnage
Makes students fear their day.
1300 dead
As shooters aim and spray.

4 of 5 had knowledge,
But failed to report.
They could have saved some lives.
Should they spend the day in court?

Guns at home and on the street
The kids know where to find.
Too easy to acquire.
Have we all lost our mind?

172 mass shooters
Most not mentally ill.
We have an epidemic,
But too many just sit still.

The NRA doesn't care
They only want the sale.
The GOP says, "So what?"
They ignore the bloody trail.

(continued)

The NRA gives ratings
To every politician.
Also contributions
Depending on their mission.

A nation weeps, people cry
Guns are loaded bullets fly'
Thousands shot, millions mourn
The NRA toots its horn.
Laws are weak, too many scorn.
A nation lost, a nation torn.

(continued)

Time

Time can be long,
Time can be short.
Sometimes we pay,
Sometimes we sort.

It can fly or lag,
Be up or drag.
An enemy or friend,
It can help us to mend.

It'll help fulfill,
But never stand still.
Can provide a thrill,
Or help us to chill.

Sometimes we need more
Sometimes we need less.
It can bring us distress.
It can bring us success.

It's the future,
The past,
It's the present,
But can't last

Often sneaks up
Cannot delay,
Unable to reason,
But can never stay.

(continued)

We watch it go by
We watch the clock.
We measure it's speed
We hear the tick tock.

Seconds or minutes,
Hours or weeks,
Months or years.
Records and streaks.

It's here, it's there
It's everywhere.
Can't be seen or stopped,
It's in the air.

It surrounds at day,
Continues at night,
Sometimes it's wrong,
But usually right

It heals, it passes,
It helps to reprieve,
It helps to perceive,
But can also deceive.

So use it wisely,
Can't get it back.
Plan ahead
And stay on track.

Their Life Cut Short

They gave us their music
They gave us their songs.
We smiled and danced
With the screaming throngs.

But they would die way too young
Way before their time.
Planes would take them down.
Still singing in their prime.

"Bye Bye Miss American Pie
The day the music died."
Holly, Valens, the Bopper
Took us on a musical ride.

Folk star Jim Croce
Gave us Leroy Brown.
And with many more top hits
'Twas his time to wear the crown.

Jim Reeves was country at its best
With his magical soothing voice
No one could quite compare,
He was mostly our first choice.

Then there was Glenn Miller
His big band and trombone.
More hits than Beattles and Elvis.
His place was on the throne.

(continued)

Van Zant and Otis Reading,
John Denver and Patsy Cline,
Ricky Nelson and Aaliyah
Were stars who each would shine.

Dozens more would perish
To or from their stage.
On there way to sing
To fans they would engage.

Their music made us smile
We'd stand and always cheer.
Their life was cut to short.
We wish they still were here.

All the Good We'll Never See

"She lived on the morning side of the mountain
And he lived on the twilight side of the hill.
They never met, they never kissed
And they will never know what they missed."

I was listening to these lyrics
The truth and sadness real.
So much out there waiting
For us to touch and feel.

All the friends we'll never meet.
All the good we'll never see.
Dances, pets and mates.
All the new that will not be.

Postscript:
An incredible song with thoughtful words and amazing vocals.
If you haven't heard Morning Side of the Mountain by
Tommy Edwards, treat yourself on google
and reflect on the lyrics of this song
and what this poem adds.

Will We Ever Be There Again?

I'm a baby boomer, I have seen it all.
Sometimes we'd crawl, sometimes stand tall.
Sometimes we'd brawl, sometimes we'd stall
Sometimes with drugs or alcohol.

What time was best in all my years?
A time of smiles and being sincere.
A time of joy to persevere.
A time of happy, loud and clear.

When I was a teen, the earth was green,
Things were keen, way more serene,
Life routine and not as mean.
There was no reason to intervene.

Schools on track,
Politicians friends
And when discord
We'd always mend.

The decades a challenge
Disappoints, mistakes
Life a maze
But we'd hit the brakes.

There was a time with much less crime.
We'd climb to the top in our prime.
No wars or fights, a time of peace.
Meals together at dinnertime.

The time was 1953
Our life was one big jolly spree
A time of glee when we were free.
Ten years of happy that we would see.

Chapter 4

School Daze
Can it really be this bad?

Schools: Close, Open, Zoom, Open, Close, Open?

Covid strikes
Covid spikes
Schools close
Learning slows.
Schools open
Close again
Teachers ill
Minds stand still
No classroom
Let's teach on zoom
Not the best
Learning repressed.
Vaccines here
Less to fear
Kids go back
Learning on track.
Omicron hits
Kid transmits
Can't unify
More will die.
No good ways
Learning strays
We look for advice
They roll the dice.

So what do we do?
They wish they knew.

Book Burning Bombshell

How could we have sunk so low
As parents curse the status quo?

They want to ban what children read
The classics, history and what they need.

"Take away, what whites have done
Let's hide the truth, their minds we'll shun."

There's answers children want to know
As curious minds seek and grow.

These answers lie in books out there
To make them grasp and be aware.

Some parents even want to burn
The books of knowledge kids will yearn.

The wonder about their bodies and more
The wonder about the civil war.
The wonder about our ancient lore
The wonder of how their minds will soar.
Their parents say they must ignore.
Their parents want to underscore.
To get their way they'll slam the door.

What about My Feelings

I'm only six can't wait for school
I'll always follow the Golden Rule.

I'll learn to read, I'll learn to write.
I'll learn to add, I'll learn to recite.

I'll get the shot, I'll wear my mask.
I'll do my lesson and stay on task.

But all I hear is parents fight.
They argue and yell over what is right.

They say no mask, but I want to wear
So I won't get sick, don't they care.

Back and forth they feud and scream,
But what about my learning dream?

Our Education in Ruins

Education not what it seems, high scores only in dreams.
Our scores nowhere near the top,
Every year they continue to drop.
Test scores tank as our teachers try,
But with their efforts we're mystified.
Unable to rectify, we only sigh and then ask why?

They give their best, but seem hard pressed.
Always stressed not to regress.
In math our rank is thirty one.

Shocked and shunned and always outdone.
Estonia, and Malta
Lativa, Taipei
Score higher than the U.S.A.

Science not better, our grades in the shredder.
I thought we were better than this.
It seems our scores continue to slip
So what can we do to get a grip?

Reading not good, we're 23rd,
What's wrong you ask this is absurb.
Every year we're outscored.
Are the students bored? Goals ignored.

So are we slow or don't we care?
We teach and study, just can't get there.
Education in ruins, we can't compete,
Tired of staying in the backseat.

So whatever it takes, make no mistake
For goodness sake there's no defeat.
Let's show some strength and not retreat.
Let's show our might and become elite.

New Word for My Students

I used to be a teacher
Who taught 5th and 6th grade,
But every year I found myself
Giving my students aid.

It came in the form of pencils
I'd give hundreds of them out.
But half way through the year
I was in a pencil drought.

I never got them back.
It should have been a loan,
But then a few days later
I'd hear their pleading tone.

They'd raise their hand and ask,
"Let me borrow once more."
I could never turn them down
So one more left my store.

Something had to be done
To make sure I got them back.
I needed to have a plan
So pencils I wouldn't lack.

So I taught a new word
What collateral meant.
It would eliminate attrition
Though my students would resent.

So when they sought a pencil
I'd ask them for a shoe
And when I got my pencil back
I'd give them theirs back too.

The Bully Solution
(I'm not kidding)

It's out of control, we need a goal.
It attacks our soul and takes a toll.

People cry, people die,
People sigh as we ask why.

At work, at play and especially school
There's always tears and fears, no golden rule.

When they bully, there's no esteem
No dreams or gleams, but silent screams.

What can we do to restrain this pain?
What can we do to contain this stain?
So far it's only been in vain
They have to know they must abstain.

I've got an idea that we should try
To get the bullies to comply.
It could pacify and unify,
It could dignify and solidify.

Instead of suspending a bully student
Let's change our intent so they'll repent.

Each school will have a room with bars
Just like jail, but with no bail.
I know this sounds quite bizarre,
But it beats the pain and growing scars.

(continued)

They'll get a warning, a wake-up call
Then off and running to bully hall.
Forget the sun, no more fun
As you sit alone in your own stall.

Other schoolmates locked away.
No time to play, to time to stray.
You're all alone in your cell.
This is home where you will dwell.

School work all day long.
No recess, friends or songs.
You'll need to learn to right your wrong.
You'll need to learn to get along.

At six o'clock your bell will sound.
It's time to get homeward bound.
But you'll be back to prison shack
Four more days to get on track.

What's in a Name?

There's one thing we all have
And that is our last name.
Some the same, some are tame
Some may lead to joy and fame.
Others are lame
But no one to blame.
We're kinda stuck,
Cannot unclaim,
It's simply going
To be part of our game.

Take for example the name I caught.
It's one I certainly would not have sought.
At times in school I got distraught.
At times I wished I could boycott.

When time for attendance I'd hear my name
Then the giggles and laughter would follow.
I'd wallow in misery, feel empty and hollow
Then take a deep breath and then a hard swallow.

My name's been Seaman for my whole life
With my woman on board when becoming my wife.

Uneasy, embarrassed
When I taught sex ed.
At times I would dread
At times turn red,
But I never lost hope
I learned to cope
To hopefully end
This slippery slope.

(continued)

Then one day I wrote my name.
Seaman appeared with its definition
"Sailor" was written next to my name.
And then I was ready for the next transition.

I than wrote "semen" on the board
Spelling its definition.
"The fluid that carries the sperm."
For everyone's recognition.

The class now knew the difference
So this is what I said:
"I'll give you 20 seconds to laugh
To get it out of your head.
Then you all will act mature,
Grown up and quite well bred!"

Postscript:
From that moment on
This plan would always work.
I never had to worry
About giggles or a smirk.

Sitting 'Round the Campfire
With Our Founding Fathers

Preface

This poem is about John Adams, James Madison,
Thomas Jefferson, Ben Franklin, Alexander Hamilton
and George Washington discussing the status of
our nation while sitting around a campfire in Heaven.

Our Founding Fathers were talkin' one day
While gathered near Heaven's Gate.
They were observing our nations woes
Knowing now we are second rate.

Jefferson said to the group,
"Our nation has taken a dive.
It no longer resembles our plan,
As their freedoms are barely alive."

James Madison loudly declared,
"They no longer compromise.
They obstruct, neglect and block
And are filled with hateful lies."

Adams talked about guns,
"It took us ten seconds to load,
Now they fire one hundred rounds,
The carnage no longer slowed."

George eagerly told his friends,
"Trump encouraged and then incited
When they stormed the House of the People
He was freed instead of indicted."

(continued)

Hamilton recalled what happened,
"The children were taken away
But when they tried to find mom and dad
All they could do was pray."

Ben told his friends 'bout voting,
"When you are standing in line
And you're thirsty and ask for water,
The law says you'll have to decline."

The group is shaking their heads
They cannot believe what they hear.
The laws and lack of compassion
Are completely insincere.

"We fought for independence,
This is not what we had in mind,
Our country is lacking in freedom.
This is not what we all signed."

When Patrick Henry spoke the words,
"Give Me Liberty or Give Me Death."
With what we have seen today
I guess he uttered his final breath.

Still Waiting

It's been a year since George Floyd died
Over a year, since justice denied
New laws attempted to be applied
But politicians unable to decide
Police brutality does not subside
America stunned and horrified.

The George Floyd law unable to pass
Our parties remain at an impasse
The police continue to attack and harass
Common sense missing, action bypassed.

The law is simple and appears to be right
Keeping knees off necks will not incite
No Knock warrants for black and white
A registry for too much might
And when cops are wrong, they will indict
This is the law that will unite.

So what's the problem for all to agree?
We need to stop this killing spree.
Civil rights must have a guarantee
No room for politics to disagree
As our nation hears our screaming plea.

The Shelves Are Bare

A manufacturer's recall
Made worse by Donald Trump
Has left baby formula
In a purchasing slump.

But President Joe Biden
Offered a plan to fix.
But the GOP members
Decided they would nix.

Republicans have said,
"No longer we'll abort
Instead we'll let them starve."
Where's the common sense court?

Wrong in So Many Ways

We broke from England, they ignored our plea.
We went to war so we'd be free.

After we won, we formed our nation
Based on freedom and legislation.

Built by leaders of their day.
But their effort fell short and we would stray.

What was promised to us was really a lie.
Our dreams of equality they would deny.

The blacks considered 3/5 of a white.
They weren't even given their own birthright.

And what about women denied the vote.
For a hundred years the men would gloat.

Everyone equal. Our leaders said no.
You see they had slaves, those wrongs they should know.

Things not swell, were they drinking that night?
Or maybe on drugs since they didn't get it right.

Postscript:
Our foundation was certainly flawed.
Not much for us to applaud.
Were our founding fathers a fraud?

What If Our Politicians Got Along?

Immigration solved, dreamers here to stay.
Taxes fair, gone the callous fray.

Voting rights equal, don't overhaul.
No more cries of fraud, each side plays ball.

New laws on guns, we all agree
Fewer dead, fewer pleas, less shooting sprees.

The choosing of judges will always be best.
No more politics, both sides impressed.

Bickering to stop, budgets in line.
Roads repaired, lying benign.

Cooperate and compromise so things get done.
We'll eat together and no longer shun.

I suddenly awake from a really weird dream
We all got along and we worked as a team.

I wished it true, but I finally took stock.
McConnell would say, "Everything we will block."

Postscript:
If only it could be like my dream
With esteem, we'd redeem, no more extreme.
No more screams, no more schemes
We'd operate now as a productive team.

Keep Politics Out

In nineteen seventy three
It became the law of the land.
In Roe versus Wade
Everyone took a stand.

Politics entered the frey.
Most Dems chose pro-choice.
The other side pro-life.
But why a political voice.

It seems it should not be
A matter for the court,
But rather a vote of all
To decide what they support.

The Lie That Killed Our Troops

When the planes hit both the Towers,
George Bush would blame Iraq.
When he tried to prove his case
The facts and proof would lack.

He spoke of massive weapons.
He assured that they were there.
Weapons of mass destruction,
His goal was wanting to scare.

Then Condoleezza Rice
Talked of a mushroom cloud.
Congress voted for war
As the lies convinced and wowed.

But no threat of nuclear arms,
No WMD's found.
No stockpiles located there.
America only frowned.

After 8 years of fighting
4000 troops had died.
100,000 civilians gone,
Because our leader lied.

I wonder how Mr. Bush
Can actually sleep at night?
He murdered thousands of souls
Just because of spite.

It's Only a Matter of Time
(Kind of a metaphor poem)

Republicans have gone too far
They've strapped explosives on their back.
It's only a matter of time
Before they detonate their pack.

When the smoldering debris has settled
And the smoke has cleared to see.
Destruction all around us
It's too late to reason and plea.

Our Constitution in ashes,
Freedom shattered and dead.
Justice now in flames
Voting rights we now shed.

Our earth is in near ruins.
Climate Change beyond our hope.
The heat and sea too hot,
We've crossed the line to cope.

We warned, we begged, we pled,
But they had their own plan.
Now too late to care
For every woman and man.

Two of a Kind

Putin murders, poisons, jails,
Attacks, assaults as he assails.
He invades a country living in peace
Unable to cope with freedom of speech.

His bombs and tanks invade Ukraine
His methods and madness inflicting pain.
His wrath betrays all that's humane.

But when Trump decides to open his mouth,
We know his brain has headed south.
The trash he spews will make us cringe
His sanity now becomes unhinged.

He refers to Putin as savvy and smart
He calls him genius, a man with heart.
There's nothing more that can be said.
Maybe the two of them should wed.

Teaching Our Children the Truth

The election's over and certified
Biden the winner in a rocky ride.
But Republicans claim their man still won
There asking for votes to be redone.
They claim fraud, but no proof to show
Sixty judges all said no.
Trump now claims he'll be reinstated
This nonsense claim is contaminated.
What kind of message does this send
How will this help our nation mend?
What will kids think when their leader lied?
When the facts are twisted and falsified.
Is this how we want our children taught?
Or would it be better if truth was sought?

Decay of Democracy

Our democracy in peril
It now slips away
They try to change the rules
On its journey to decay.

They dishonor and disgrace.
They delay, then debase,
They demean, they degrade,
Disgust, disobey.
Disregard, won't debate,
Discount, denigrate,
Disable and dictate.
Disagree, desecrate.

The GOP so strong
It's time for goodbyes
Trying for the truth
But too many lies.

I Live in a Country Where.........

I live in a country where a President was impeached
twice and received 74 million votes.

I live in a country where the President said on television
if we drink bleach it might protect us against the covid virus.

I live in a country where the President's administration took illegal
immigrant children from their parents and were unable to reunite many
of them
because they could not locate the parents.

I live in a country where 60 judges ruled there was no fraud in
the 2020 election, but 70% of Republicans still believe their candidate
won.

I live in a country where the President
has told over 22,000 lies or mistruths in his 4 year term.

I live in a country where the President lied and
committed treason to promote the storming of the U. S. Capitol.

I live in a country where the President pardoned
convicted criminals of serious crimes, many of them his friends.

I live in a country where the President called an African country a
shithole place.

I live in a country where the President praised hate groups.

I live in a country where the President wanted to reduce
covid testing so he could minimize the number of reported cases.

(continued)

I live in a country where many voted for Trump because they wanted a President with strong business knowledge even though he had filed for bankruptcy 6 times.

I live in a country where this President may
run in 2024 with a strong possibility of winning.

What Do You See in the Mirror?

What do Republican leaders see
When looking in the mirror?
Do they see one who's always fair?
Could their life be any clearer?

But what do they really see?
Are they deceiving every day?
What do they really feel?
When truth continues to stray.

They stare and glare at the glass.
Do they think they're being true?
Do they understand the ethics?
Do they even have a clue?

They misrepresent and lie
They break promises they made.
They falsify and fabricate
There is no help or aid.

Are they capable of love?
How do they sleep at night?
What do they say to God?
When they know they're seldom right.

Nothing Like T.V. and a Good Meal To Watch People Getting Beaten Up

The attack on our Capitol
Is still on our mind
Instead of stopping
Our President dined.

His personal staff
Asked him to stop.
But when he ignored
There was a dead cop.

His family would plead
For him to end.
But he continued to watch
And would not bend.

Many were hurt
And some even died.
He continued to watch
As he still denied.

One phone call
Was all it would take.
To end this treason
And our heartache.

Our freedom on pause,
Constitution at stake.
Democracy waning
While Trump took a break.

Is This Democracy?

Politicians campaign, they plead their case.
They hope to sway and build a base.

The people choose when they cast their votes,
They hope their dreams the winner promotes.

But when in Congress they'll present a bill,
But it's not that easy on Capitol Hill.

The Senate leader has a choice.
He may decide to silence their voice.

He may not bring the bill to the floor.
He alone, can choose to ignore.

So in that case the people's needs
Will be ignored by one man's deeds.

One man decides if we should hear
One man decides should it disappear.

So we must ask if this is fair
One man alone may not care.

Are the people heard when they select
Or can one man choose to scorn and neglect.

Is this the freedom that we fought for?
Is this the dream we had in store?

The $5.00 Ladder

A campaign promise by Trump
Was to build a border wall.
He said Mexico would pay,
But they said no to install.

Eleven billion was the cost
Twenty million per each mile.
The most expensive in the world,
Was the cost really worthwhile?

Trump continued to promise
No cost to the U. S. A.
They finally started to build,
But Mexico said no way.

Thirty feet of steel
Thirty feet to sprout
Thirty feet to hamper
To keep illegals out.

So Trump continued to build,
But ladders would be found.
They only cost five bucks.
Discarded on the ground.

This just goes to show
If you do not want to stay
And you need to cross the border
You'll always find a way.

Backwards

Millions of years to evolve
For us to become who we are.
Millions of years of changes
To finally reach the bar.

But Repubs are going backward
As they've changed our institution.
Their brain cells now dissolving
As they practice reverse evolution.

They no longer act like humans
Their actions show they're numb.
They'll soon become an amoeba
Which is where we all came from.

100 Years of Disgrace
200 Tries of Shame

Some things we see we cannot grasp
Some things we hear we only gasp.
There're so horrific we can't believe.
They're so appalling we can't conceive.

It took one hundred years to pass.
Too few votes they would amass.
Two hundred tries to get a law.
The Southern states would keep the flaw.

A time so vile, left us in shock.
A time of shame, how could they block?
Defies what's right to keep this wrong.
Compassion gone for way too long.

So what's this lurking evil plight?
One hundred years to see the light.
Barbaric times we lynched a soul.
One hundred years it took its toll.

They took the law into their hands.
They'd lynch a man throughout the lands.
No trial or judge, only a tree,
A horse, a branch and empty plea.

One hundred years, Two hundred tries
To pass a law to legalize,
No more lynching's, no more cries
The minds in Congress mystifies.

Our History Books Must Be Wrong

My grandkids now in school.
When they open up their book
The history is so horrid
Their minds are really shook.

Their history book will say
That Trump put kids in cages.
But when they could not find their parents
Our country faced outrages.

Trump would also side
With groups promoting hate.
He wouldn't condemn their views,
But would rather validate.

When our Capitol was seized,
He encouraged their attack.
He refused to call in troops
And simply turned his back.

They wanted to shoot Pelosi.
They wanted to hang Pence.
Trump didn't seem to care
As police were on defense.

They couldn't believe the words
They were reading on the page.
This history filled with horror
Their minds were filled with rage!

(continued)

He ruled using fear.
His party was afraid.
So they let him have his way
As our nation soon decayed.

They must be reading fiction.
The reader can't conceive.
These facts cannot be true.
How can anyone believe?

Separated

When I was born there was joy and glee
I remember sitting on my father's knee.

I learned to crawl and then to walk.
Soon there were words and I could talk.

We lived in a country of militia and thugs
With dangerous cartels and rampant drugs.

My parents said we could not stay
So we left our home for the USA.

We hiked and climbed with hunger pains
But we kept alive by the freedom of gains.

We crossed the border, but soon were caught
That feeling was one of defeat and distraught.

We were split apart, I was sent away'
Unable to smile or laugh or play.

I'd see barbed wire when I looked to the sky.
I miss my parents and I start to cry.

They call our home a detention camp
The beds too short, the floor too damp.

After a year they did what was right
They looked for parents so we could unite.

But hundreds of parents could not be found
So I had to stay in the caged compound.

My parents are gone, I'm all alone
I'm only eight and on my own.

What Happened to the Vote for Truth?
(On Insurrection Day)

Politics can surprise the masses
As our elected officials behave like asses.
But I never saw them stoop so low
Until they told Ms, Sicknick NO!

She is the mom of Brian who died
Protecting Republicans so they could hide.
She went to the Capitol so she could talk
To visit Republicans, but they would walk.

Her son gave his life while saving theirs,
But it seems these cowards did not care.
She was only seeking their vote for truth
But instead they were rude and quite uncouth.

That day that Gladys was snubbed and ignored
Their souls escaped and went out the door.

Postscript
After concerns, assassinations or war
There's always commissions to dig and explore
But this time the Republicans would choose to ignore
Afraid it would change the election score.
Red or Blue, rich or poor, our nation's integrity we need to restore.

Trump's Legacy

January six we were attacked by our own.
Our sacred Capital looked like a war zone.

Days before, Trump would yell,
Our election a fraud, let's fight like hell.

He incited, encouraged and lied to his crowd.
The insurgents gathered and they were wowed.

They stormed and fought and they were armed.
Their chants and threats were laced with harm.

They threatened Pelosi who they wanted to kill.
She became their bullseye just for the thrill.

They threatened to hang Trump's V.P.
As the Senators and others scrambled to flee.

Too few cops to curtail their rush.
Some would die and others were crushed.

A hundred and forty were hurt in the fight.
The throngs of evil had too much might.

The battle raged on and would not cease.
Covid would strike thirty eight police.

Troops not called, nowhere to be seen.
No calls from Trump to intervene.

Seemed like treason and they voted to impeach.
But the Senate feared Trump, so the votes wouldn't reach.

(continued)

The right thing to do was blocked by fright,
Justice ignored, replaced by spite.

But history will show that Trump paid the price.
The only President to be impeached twice.

Standing Still

This is what happens when we stand still
The crazies get guns and go out and kill
Republicans refuse to pass a bill.
They ignore and neglect and continue to chill.

The following occurred in a weekend in May
Thirteen mass shootings, the innocent pay.
Thirteen dead as the bullets spray,
Seventy hurt as the wounded lay.

So what can be done to stop this turn.
This carnage should spark an immediate concern
By now you'd think they should have learned
Too many tears, we still yearn.

What's Happened to Integrity

When we elect our leader, they should always be
Above all the rest to serve you and me.

But since I've been voting, that's not been the case.
Absent trust and honor and showing no grace.

Kennedy was good, but strayed from his wife.
Too many flings, not a loyal married life.

Johnson then took over, unable to end the war.
He cheated on his wife so much, it was hard to keep score.

Followed by Tricky Dick and the break in at Watergate.
Hearings, tapes and shame and soon it was checkmate.

Then it was Ronald Reagan's turn, he would favor the well to do.
His trickle down economy was a terrible miscue.

Senior George Bush broke a promise that he made,
"No new taxes, was a pledge that he betrayed."

Next was Clinton, he proved okay,
But too many affairs caused him to stray.

Enter the other Bush, too many G. I.'s died
We fought the wrong enemy, our nation grieved and cried.

Barack Obama followed, making history on the way.
He showed us each empathy and made us proud each day.

Not too much to celebrate, most dishonored our sacred trust.
How could we misjudge that most would be a bust.

Careful When You Place the Blame

Every four years we vote
To elect our President.
The people listen and choose
And then they give consent.

But after several months
Their performance sometimes fades.
The polls reflect their job
With very low passing grades.

But is this really fair
For them to get the blame?
There's only so much they can do
So let's hold back the shame.

The other party may attack.
The other side may block.
They'll lie and cheat, no middle ground
Resulting in gridlock.

The nation blames their leader,
But he does nothing wrong.
He doesn't make the laws,
But he tries to get along.

He attempts to compromise.
He seeks to energize.
He strives to improvise.
He tries to sympathize.
He undertakes to harmonize.

But the nation doesn't get
Sometimes his hands are tied.
It takes both sides to get it done
For us to take this ride.

I Think They've Got it Backwards

Thirteen Repubs vote to pass,
But then their members would harass.

The bill would benefit all of us.
There should not be any fuss.

But the GOP wants to punish them
For doing their job they will condemn.

But Congressman Gosar's video would share
Depicts him killing a Dem, beware.

He would not receive any condemnation
Or discussion of censure or termination.

Seems like a double standard to me.
The party cannot be so carefree.

The GOP needs to keep in sight.
To do what's fair and get it right!

How Long Would You Wait
In Line for Freedom

The Republicans lost the Senate
And the lower Chamber too.
And when they lost the White House
They knew what they had to do.

They made it harder to vote,
They changed election laws.
They took away our freedom
We're now a nation of flaws.

Some states even took away
The right to mail your vote.
Fewer hours polls are open
Precincts few and remote.

So to keep our freedom alive
How long would you wait in line?
Would you stand for half a day
Or go home to dine and play?

By the Numbers

Over 19,000 people were killed in shootings and firearm related events
in 2020.

23 unarmed blacks were fatally shot by police in 2018

70 judges ruled there was no fraud in the 2020 election yet 76% of
Republicans
believe there was widespread fraud in a February 2021 poll.

There are 917 hate groups in America

Over 100 million adults said they would not wear a mask during a
surge
In the covid pandemic

There were 5 deaths and 138 police injured when our Capitol was
attacked on
January 6th, but some Republicans referred to the insurrection as a
normal tourist
day at the Capitol.

74 million people voted to re-elect Donald Trump even though he was
a
self proclaimed racist.

3600 healthcare workers died from the covid virus while saving
the lives of patients who killed them.

38 million Americans live in poverty.

Over 550,000 people are homeless.

In 2016 there were 2,418,352 inmates.

And people say we live in the greatest nation on earth.

Chapter 6

Family, Friends and Pets
It's All About Love

Fate at Its Best
A Special Journey Down My Hallway
A Special Place on My Pillow
Make That Call
Transformation
Say It Now
A Karen Sighting
Understanding Dog Bark
Mom's Day 2022

Fate at Its Best

I went to Arizona State
Where I planned to learn and graduate.
But then one day there entered fate.
This girl's face would radiate.
Her presence would illuminate
Which caused my heart to palpitate.
And soon my being to exhilarate.
It didn't take long to gravitate.
Our feelings soon would stimulate.
And then our love would escalate.
Our souls together would integrate.
We'd laugh when we we'd communicate.
And then one day we changed the slate.
Her last name she would liquidate.
With Rabbi and friends we'd celebrate.
And a few years later we'd populate.

A Special Journey Down My Hallway

One day when I came home from work
I walked through my front door.
But I could not help to see
What was sitting on the floor.

In front of where I stood
Rose peddles staring at me.
They formed a path down the hall
So I followed the peddle spree.

Down the hallway I went
Following the red delight.
The peddles made a turn
Then I saw a loving sight.

The peddles climbed onto the bed
My wife was wearing a smile.
That's all that she had on.
So I'll get back to you in a while.

A Special Place on My Pillow

If you really love your dog
You'll take him to the park.
You'll train, reward and pet him
And understand his bark.

You'll let him on the couch
You'll let him on the bed
You'll take him in the car
And you'll keep him well fed.

But there's a special kind of love
When it's time to go to sleep.
Invite him on your pillow
And together you'll count sheep.

Make That Call

We all make friends, some lifelong,
But sometimes they fade away.
But now it's time to reconnect
And contact those who stray.

Don't wait for them to call,
It's best you take the lead.
Don't put off 'til later,
It's time that you proceed.

So grab the phone and dial up
There's joy in hearing their voice.
Forget a message or a text,
The phone is your first choice.

You say that you're not sure.
Too much time gone by.
But that's a better reason
For you to justify.

Transformation

Oh, he's so adorable
Look at all that hair.
He looks just like dad
Family, friends declare.

Mother and son bond
When mom needs to feed.
They rock together in the chair
As dad gets a book to read.

Soon there is a smile
He's crawling all around.
He even starts to laugh
And gains another pound.

Things are going great
And soon he starts to walk.
His hair is getting longer
And then we hear him talk.

He made us feel proud
With a lemonade stand.
He was always kind to others
Giving a helping hand.

But then he fell apart.
This isn't what we planned
He's now hostile and mean.
We do not understand.

(continued)

He chose the path to drugs
And abused alcohol.
He dropped out of school
And spent time in juvi hall.

Mom and Dad asked themselves
"Where did we go wrong?
We taught our son values
And how to get along."

But peers can grab their soul.
They need to stand and show.
They're able to walk away
Be strong and just say no!

Say It Now

You need to tell your friends
They're important in your life.
Parents, kids and others
And your husband and your wife.

Even though they know,
Those words must be heard.
It sends feelings of love
So don't let it be inferred.

A note, a call, in person
Or an impromptu letter.
Go the extra mile
Sending roses would be better.

Don't wait too long or hesitate.
You may find it is too late.
They need to hear it now
That you appreciate.

A Karen Sighting

You wonder when you'll meet her
The perfect girl for you.
You wonder what she'll look like
But you do not have a clue.

The first time I saw Karen
It was at her college dorm.
Little did I know
That my life would be transformed.

Her smile, eyes and hair
Swept me off my feet.
And on our first date
You could hear my heart beat.

As she walked down the stairs
I was frozen where I stood.
Could this be just a dream?
Could it really be this good?

Flash forward fifty years
It was surely not a dream.
Our life was meant to be
"Cause we're the perfect team."

Mom's Day
2022

Another year and May is here
So happy day to Karen dear.
The best mom ever, it's crystal clear
The best mom ever on the hemisphere.

Year after year you're always there
For kids and pets you always care.
Your breed is special and very rare.
You're very loving, you always share.

So here's a poem from me to you
To praise my wife for all you do.
You operate with no curfew.
You get it done as if on cue.

You wash and dry and dust and clean.
You wax and polish till there's a sheen.

You feed the dog, pick up his poop.
And when we're sick there's chicken soup.

You cook our meals then clean the mess.
Always smiling while you finesse.

You feed the cat, give him a treat.
And every day you will repeat.

You vac the rug and sweep the floors.
And wipe the dog when it pours.

You rake the leaves and clean the yard.
And you never use the credit card.

(continued)

You'll always clean and flush the litter.
You're also happy and never bitter.

You water plants and clean the car.
You're nothing short of a super star.

Postscript:

Is Karen really this good you ask?
Can anyone be this much on task?

Sometimes a poet may stretch a bit
To get the poem to rhyme and fit.

But the answer is she is that good,
Nominated for sainthood.

Understanding Dog Bark

I heard my dog trying to speak
And since I understood his bark
He said to me, "Please Dad
Can you take me to the park?"

Most cities have a park for dogs
Surrounded by a fence.
The dogs can run with friends
And sniff around their scents.

There is no leash required
So the dogs can run and chase.
Retrieve, swim and visit
They'll find no better place.

As an owner of a dog
This is something we must do.
Their happiness will bring a smile
So find a park near you.

Postscript:
Be careful where you step,
Watch your rendezvous.
Keep your eyes down low
To avoid a pile of poo.

Who is This Person?

Her sincerity flows from all her pores.
Her compassion travels from her inner core.
Her stature we certainly all adore.
Her charm contagious and evermore.
Her fun and humor a downpour.
Her respect is special, cannot ignore
Enthusiasm more than you could hope for.
Her willingness always gets an encore.
Her smarts achieve the highest score.
Her adventureness always to explore.
Her determination a tug of war.
She's everyone's friend and mentor.
When I met Karen my life would soar.
With Laughter, Love and Fun Galore!

Chapter 7

Humor
A Little Comic Relief

The Dilemma of Bread
The Losing Battle
How Trump Got Things Done
The Right to Bear Arms
The Saga of Toilet Paper
To Fit or Not to Fit

The Dilemma of Bread

My wife was craving a sandwich one night
But we had run out of bread.
So I went to the store to buy her a loaf.
When I return she'll be well fed.

I parked the car and went inside
Headed for the bread aisle.
I wasn't prepared for what I saw
No longer able to smile.

My eyes went to whole grain
With choices of different seeds.
Five or nine, 22 or more
Made it difficult for me to proceed.

What about raison or pita
Or French, Italian or rye?
Maybe sour dough or garlic.
The store could now hear me sigh.

I was leaning toward getting the rye,
But the choice became harder to fill.
Should it be Jewish or marbled
Or light or dark or dill?

Maybe the one with honey
Or sprouted or just plain wheat.
And then when I saw the potato
My anxiety said let's retreat.

(continued)

Buttermilk, Hawaiian or Naan,
Cinnamon, or the wheat berry.
Maybe I'll get the focaccia
Or one with herbs and rosemary.

How 'bout the challah or Keto?
Should it be gluten free?
What about bagels or rolls?
Another choice for my Sweet Pea.

Should it be sliced or whole?
Should it be thick or thinner?
I was practically out of my mind
When I came home with a T.V. dinner.

The Losing Battle

I couldn't quite finish the meal
So I reached for the plastic wrap
I needed to cover the leftovers,
But could not find the open flap.

I searched and tried to separate.
Unable to find the end.
I removed the roll from the box,
But no plastic would descend.

I finally found the seam,
But could not get it to slide.
I gently pulled the wrap,
But it stuck and would not glide.

I finally got the right amount,
I had a perfect square.
I slid my arm to get the cut
And was ready for the tear.

But then it did its thing.
No longer flat and square.
It twisted, turned and slid
All I could do was swear.

So I reached to smooth it out.
I pulled each side with grace.
Back and forth, right and left
To get it back in place.

It seemed a losing fight,
Way too much turmoil.
So I rolled it in a ball
And grabbed the aluminum foil.

How Trump Got Things Done

Four years of Trump was quite a ride.
Most know he wasn't qualified.
His lack of leading would divide.
Our nation's progress would subside.

I wondered what made Donald tick.
I wondered why he was so slick.
Still so many felt his click.
Was he unstable, was he sick?

It took a while to figure out.
What Donald Trump was all about.
How America hit a drought.
Why we'd cry, why we'd shout.

When something needed to get done.
Advice from others he ignored.
Instead he'd open up his drawer
And grab his trusty Ouija board.

Sometimes he'd get the deck
When staff would disregard.
To help him find the way,
He'd use a Tarot card.

And when unsure of what to do
He'd touch his crystal ball.
He'd always honor what it said
When seeking truth for all.

(continued)

When having a leader visit
And things were at a low.
To get on track, they'd play
A game of tic tac toe.

Sometimes he'd spin a spinner
Wanting to be precise.
And if he still was not sure
He'd grab a pair of dice.

And when confronting evil
And things were really foul
To rid the evil spirits
He'd stick pins in a doll.

So now we know his style
To help us understand.
What makes Donald tick?
As we enter fairyland.

The Right to Bear Arms
(A Parody)

I decided to increase my arsenal.
The Constitution says it's right.
One day there may be a robber
That I'll need to confront in the night.

So I purchased a missle launcher
And a bazooka to cover my flank.
I added a mighty flame thrower
And a brand new Sherman Tank.

Then a combat machine gun
On the roof of my new car.
I wanted to be prepared
While driving by my bar.

Since I have the right to bear arms,
I knew I'd be okay.
I just hoped my schizophrenia
Won't cause it to get in the way.

The Saga of Toilet Paper

During the covid virus
I'm trying to figure out.
Why no toilet paper?
What caused this shopping drought.

The shelves were bare, I do declare.
We all would swear and go elsewhere.
We hoped to snare, but nothing there.
This wasn't fair, we said a prayer.
They did not care, they would not share.
We could not bear, we pulled our hair.
Beware of panic in the air.
Unaware of this nightmare.
Could not prepare for this warfare.
It was worse than sitting in a dentist chair.

To Fit or Not to Fit

I went to the mall one day
To go on a shopping spree.
I needed to buy some clothes,
But the size would disagree.

I tried them on in the dressing room,
But they were a little tight.
So I got a larger size,
But they still didn't fit quite right.

I thought the larger size
Probably would shrink.
If I washed them in hot water
I'd be okay I'd think.

So when I got home I cut the label
And put them in the wash.
I turned the dial to hot
And heard the water slosh.

Then into the dryer they went.
The dial set to extra heat
And I gave it extra time
As I added the dryer sheet.

I couldn't wait to see the fit
When the dryer noise had stopped.
I was hoping the heat had worked
And that extra size had dropped.

But when I tried them on
I saw my plan had sunk.
They still were large on me
'Cause the label said pre-shrunk.

Chapter 8

Miscellaneous
A Little Bit of This
A Little Bit of That

Rainbows
Bigger Than Life
Second Chances
What Makes Me Tick
One Very Special Evening

Rainbows

Sadness in the sky,
Tears flutter to the ground.
What my eyes behold
As colors head earthbound.

A palette held by arms of clouds
Reaching out to brush.
Up and down they stroke
In mutual tones of hush.

The beauty comes from all that's good,
The red in cherry pies.
The ocean blue and fresh mowed lawn
And the moon which glorifies.

A bouquet of violet flowers,
A sunset with its glow.
The winds will blow into an arc
With the last one indigo.

The colors disappear.
They don't hang around to gloat.
Maybe what they need
Is another heavy coat.

Bigger Than Life

This poem is quite different than the other 300
I have written. Its purpose is for the reader to take a
trip through history and reconnect with the individuals
that made our world what it was and what it has become.

Most are in our history books
Like Churchill and Marco Polo.
All are famous for what they've done
Like Charles De Gaulle and Plato.

Some were good and others not
Like Rosa Parks and Castro,
But all were bigger than life
Like Henry Ford and Picasso.

The Babe and Lewis and Clark
FDR and Disney
Mother Teresa and Elvis
And Leonardo da Vinci.

Armstrong, Gable, Salk,
Dr. Seuss and Michael Jackson,
Pasteur, Gates and The Beattles,
Abe and Thomas Edison.

Jesus Christ and Moses,
Columbus and Madonna,
Celine Dion and Oprah,
Mandela and Dalia Lama.

(continued)

Hitchcock, Freud and Trump,
Liz Taylor, Pele, Homer
The Wright Brothers and Beethoven
John Lewis and Arnold Palmer.

RBG and Einstein
Thatcher, Ike and Gandhi
Thurgood Marshall and Wilt
And the great Muhammed Ali

Desmond Tutu and Van Gogh
Zuckerberg and Lenin
Ronald Reagan and Lindy
Captain Sully and Charles Darwin.

Wyatt Earp and Earhardt
Stephen King and Stalin,
Florence Nightingale
Shakespeare and Ben Franklin.

Beyonce and the Queens
John Wayne and Madam Currie
King Tut and all the Popes
Bezos and McCarthy.

Alexander Graham Bell,
Diana and Grace Kelly
Malcolm X and Putin
Tom Hanks and Pavoratti.

Sitting Bull and Caesar
Marx and Charlie Chaplin,
Elton John and Hitler
Paul Revere and Marilyn

(continued)

Frank Lloyd Wright and Keller
Dolly and Dr. King
Jefferson and Koby
Mark Twain, Mao and Sting

Meryl Streep and Warhol,
Joan of Arc and JFK,
Daniel Boone and Dylan,
Cher and Hemingway.

Michael Phelps and Jacqueline
O. J. and Lady Ga Ga,
James Dean and General Patton,
Bob Hope and Barrack Obama

Jackie Robinson and Ness
Issac Newton and Houdini
Confuses and Napolean
Nixon and Mancini

Second Chances

Sometimes the title says it all.
Special words that say no more.
No need to even write the poem,
Just read, react and don't ignore!

What Makes Me Tick

I thought I would take stock
And write what makes me tick.
I like to watch movies
Including a chick flick'

I always do my best
Wanting to achieve
I love taking pictures
I'd rather give than receive.

I've always worked hard,
But know the need to play.
I've always been a maverick
And sought a better way.

I like to play games
I feel others pain.
I like to treat myself.
I'm afraid to fly in planes.

I satisfy my cravings
It's okay if I cry.
I love teaching children
I hate to wear a tie.

I keep things in order
I fear snakes and spiders
I like to read books
And I'm a pretty fair writer.

(continued)

I always use logic.
I always think things through.
Common sense is more important
Then a really high I.Q.

I don't like giving up,
But know when to move on.
I'd rather go to the store
Than shop at Amazon.

It's important that I laugh,
I like when others smile.
I always ask questions,
And I go the extra mile.

I write books and poems.
I keep priorities straight.
I like to cook meals
And I believe in fate.

I like to have fun.
I don't wait for one to call.
I remember mom and dad
I love to shop the mall.

I download favorite songs.
I love going to the gym.
I like camping in my tent.
I do things on the whim.

Everyone has a bio
Everyone has to click.
Everyone is special.
So what makes you all tick?

One Very Special Evening

It was a Hot August Night
In '72.
An audience eager to hear
The songs, lyrics and melodies
Watching through the stars
Captivated by the magic and aura of the Greek.
Breathtaking anticipation
As the instruments came to life
And Neil Diamond stepped onto the stage.
The audience mesmerized,
Eyes transfixed,
Ears straining,
Voices screaming,
Hands coming together
Over and over.
A night etched in memory,
A mystique awakened in our soul
An evening reaching its climax
With Soolamon and Brother Love's Traveling Salvation Show
"All God's Children"
Realizing
Something hypnotic
Something special.
Nothing like it before.
Nothing like it since.

Chapter 9

Favorites

From my first book:
"Partly Sunny with a Chance of Laughter"

Colors
Pasta-bilities
Ode to Zoo Keepers
My Journey
On Empty
Imprisoned
Tears
The Learning Puzzle
Resume of Life
Can Freedom Be Bought
Relief
My Corner
Burning Question
Wealth
December 10th

Colors

There's so much beauty in colors,
But which do you think the best?
The one that's most impactful
And stands above all the rest?

The beautiful orange sunset,
Or the blue in our lakes and sky?
The yellow we see as we gaze at the moon,
Or the red in a cherry pie?

Then there's the spectrum of browns
We admire in so many places.
A gorge or canyon or peak
And a world of so many faces.

The white of a snow capped mountain
The gold in a field of wheat.
The turquoise in a rare gem
Or the lime of a popsicle treat.

Now there's a color that's rather bland.
It will not excite your eyes.
But it's special in what it does
As it helps to compromise.

There's many who only see
The world in black or white.
But it's hard for trust to exist
In this non-productive light.

When we get stubborn and cannot agree,
And no longer want to try
Let's paint the world in shades of gray
Then maybe we'll see eye to eye.

Pasta-bilities

I was in the mood for pasta one day
So went to the Italian Deli.
I knew what they had would satisfy
My pasta-craving belly.

I knew there was quite an assortment,
I'd been to this deli before.
The pasta aisle stretched all the way
To the very back of the store.

The first one that I saw
Looked like miniature bow ties,
But as I ambled down the aisle
I saw every shape and size.

Twists and cones and tubes,
Coils and wagon wheels.
So many kinds to choose
To plan my family meals.

Hats, ribbons and curlicues,
Some in the shape of straws.
I was getting overwhelmed
For a minute I had to pause.

One looked like a mushroom
Another looked like a horn.
Impossible to decide,
I was starting to feel forlorn.

(continued)

Caravelle, Campanelle and one called fettucelle,
Cavatelli, gemelli, anelli and vermicelli.
Tripolini, bucatini and stuffed tortellini,
Spiralini, ditalini, tubini and rotini.

I couldn't pronounce the names
When I reached for the capelletti.
It came in the shape of a hat
But I decided to change to rocchetti.

By now I was such a wreck,
I couldn't decide a thing.
So I left the store, started my car
And drove to Burger King.

Postscript:
There's one thing I don't get
In the pasta hall of fame.
Why are there so many shapes
When they all taste the same?

Ode to Zoo Keepers

(This poem was written by Karen when she was working at the Los Angeles
Zoo as a keeper)

We are the keepers
A quite elite group.
We spend our days looking
For something to scoop.
With bucket in hand
And shovel and rake,
We're so dedicated
We make no mistake.
We're especially careful
To pile up the poo,
From antelope, zebra,
Springbok and gnu.
The monkeys and apes
Will make us most happy
When we look in their cages
And find something crappy.
We enter exhibits
And clean up the feces
Of lions and tigers
And endangered species.
We enter the flight cage
And rake up the turds
Of both ordinary
And exotic birds.
We come in each morning
And pull on our boots
Then wade in the droppings
Of mallards and coots.

And then in the P. M.
We tackle the B. M.

My Journey

As I grew up I longed to feel
That God was there for me.
But my mind was clouded with so much doubt
His presence was hard to see.

So much misery, pain and strife,
Suffering, anguish and grief.
I'd cry out to God and ask Him "Why?"
So stuck in disbelief.

All that I saw in humanity
Was bigotry, hate and greed.
It was hard for me to believe He's here,
But I desperately felt the need.

The innocent dying before their time
And the millions that perish in war.
I looked around and shook my head.
What was all this destruction for?

The older I got the more I needed
To clearly be shown a sign.
I begged out loud to be convinced
I was His and He was mine.

Though affirmation never came,
I continued to seek Him out.
And then one day I finally knew
What God was all about.

(continued)

I wasn't sure I had faith enough,
But I felt I had really come far.
I'd have been happy to leave it there,
But God kept raising the bar.

I could no longer look around
Without seeing His hand in all.
And His spirit alive in so many,
Though we sometimes stumble and fall.

The beauty of nature, the strength of hope,
The ability to logically think
Says there is more to it than Darwin
And God is the missing link.

Maybe when all is said and done,
The question should really be:
Not "do I believe in God?"
But "does God believe in me?"

On Empty

My life now runs on empty;
My will to live is gone;
I cry myself to sleep at night
And dread the coming dawn.

I seem invisible at school;
No friends to call my own.
I sit at lunchtime by myself
I'm always all alone

No phone calls ever come to me
And dates are just a dream.
No one wants to be my friend
Or choose me for the team.

My hair is always frizzy,
My skin is never clear.
My body slightly overweight,
They all just laugh and jeer.

I've never been unkind at all,
I've never picked a fight.
I don't know why it goes so wrong
When I've tried to make it right.

I stand here contemplating
As my tears fall down like rain.
Why do they get such pleasure
From a lonely person's pain?

Postscript:
*I have read this poem dozens of times, and
continue to always shed tears because it is so
real to so many.*

Imprisoned

I stood inside my box
As if I were in jail.
I'm just like all the others
We all are doomed to fail.

I wanted to be different
Unique and fancy free.
I was desperate to escape
So I could be just me.

I looked around to find a key
That would open the sealed door.
I needed to step out so that
My life I could explore.

I pleaded for my freedom,
I knew I had to flee.
For kicks, I simply turned the knob
It opened! I was free!

I now can live my life
A bit unorthodox.
Because I opened up that door
To think outside the box.

Tears

(This poem is about a song on a CD titled
"Jay and the Americans Greatest Hits"
and how it affected me.)
(Jim)

I was driving my car to work one day
When I reached for my new CD.
I was very relaxed and happy,
Not a worry and quite carefree.

I pushed the disc into the slot
And turned the volume to high.
A few songs later the group sang one
That was titled "Hushabye".

It seemed rather strange to me
That this song became a rock hit.
An older song for young children
Did not seem like a very good fit.

I listened to the words of this new song.
And was touched by this lullabye.
Then something surprising happened to me
I broke down and started to cry.

So I played the song again and again,
Waiting for the words I'd hear.
And then it happened just as before,
Had to wipe away a tear.

(continued)

It happened over and over
No matter my mood or season
I tried to think of why this should be,
But could not come up with a reason.

At first I thought it was personal,
But I couldn't remember the song.
Maybe something in my early years?
But that just felt all wrong.

I loved this song and listened a lot,
But always continued to cry.
I had no answer for my tears
Just kept on wondering why.

Then one day I suddenly knew
What made me feel this way.
And why I was always moved to tears
Each time this song would play.

Sometimes when children are born,
It's an uphill climb with pain.
Single moms and foster care,
Neglect and financial strain.

Latch-key kids, low self-esteem,
The struggle to stay off drugs.
Mothers and fathers splitting up
And the lure of gangs and thugs.

And the older they grow, the more pressure
As they strive to get along
Not all of them will have the help
They need to grow up strong.

(continued)

So when I hear the song now,
I know just why I cry
Not every child's life will be
A loving lullabye.

The Learning Puzzle
(All the Pieces Must Fit)

They all start school at an early age,
To one day thrive and earn a good wage.

They learn about math and how to write
They become better readers and learn to recite.

Science and health, history and more.
Their skills develop, their minds will soar.

As they learn, they mature and grow,
But there's one more thing they need to know.

The one thing lacking that isn't taught
Is probably not what you would have thought.

We need to teach them to hope and dream,
To blossom with promise and self-esteem.

To succeed in life each woman or man
Must first believe they truly can.

Resume of Life

You're born, you grow, you change
You adapt, adjust, and refine.
Your life is full of twists and turns
It's a journey before you'll shine.

Every good. every bad, every choice
Will give you another clue.
Every up, every down, every step
Starts to mold you into you.

You marry, divorce, and fall
You bully, you fight, you cheat.
But soon you'll find the way
And you're right back on your feet.

You're fired, alone, and hurt
You don't know where you should turn.
But with every painful struggle
There's a lesson you will learn.

And as you grow and conquer
You'll deal with all this strife,
You see, you have been writing
Your resume of life.

Can Freedom Be Bought?

There was a knock on the door that came late at night.
I opened it up to a frightening sight.
The first thing I saw were guns aimed at me
When I heard someone say, "Don't attempt to flee."

They pushed their way in and I soon realized,
They were uniformed cops and became paralyzed.
I was afraid and confused and unable to speak
When they read me my rights my knees went weak.

I was pushed to the wall and patted down.
They were looking for weapons, but none would be found.
I next felt the metal, circling my wrists.
My fear spread to anger as I clenched both my fists.

I needed to know what I did so abhorrent.
My nightmare began when I saw their warrant.
It said I had robbed a convenience store,
And had used a gun when I walked through the door.

I was taken downtown to the county jail
And when I saw the bars, my face went pale.
I was soon fingerprinted and put in a cell
And I knew at that moment I had entered hell.

I knew I was innocent but with my arrest,
I needed a lawyer and I needed the best.
I was stone-cold broke and my only way
Was a public defender I would not have to pay.

(continued)

He came the next day to discuss my trial,
But when I heard what he said, I disliked his style.
With no alibi and the witness they had,
I began to lose faith and my future looked bad.

I believe my attorney thought I did the crime
And he said if convicted, I would do hard time.
I pleaded to him that it was not me,
But he thought it was best to cop to a plea.

My answer was "No!" and I became defiant.
I told him I was innocent and to fight for his client.
He was lacking experience and underpaid
With too many files and not enough aid.

He bounced back and forth from case to case.
No adequate time with his hurried pace.
And then it was time to see the judge.
But when he heard the evidence, he would not budge.

When I heard the word "guilty" tears rolled down my face.
And then the judge said, "Let's hear the next case."
If I only had money for a lawyer's fee,
He may have done better and I would be free.

Relief

My wife had a cold and a headache
And needed a cure for the pain.
So I told her I'd drive to the store
To prevent an impending migraine.

I went straight to the aisle with remedies
Thinking this would really be quick.
I wanted to get the right one
So my wife would stop feeling so sick.

I started to reach for the Tylenol
When my eyes gazed left and then right.
What I saw on the shelves all around me
Was a very confusing sight.

I saw the Bayer, Advil and Aleve,
And Excedrin next to the Anacin.
I wondered about one called Orudis
When I decided to change to the Motrin

This was harder than I thought it would be,
When I spotted the Pamprin and the Nuprin.
They were above the Percogesic
And below the Bufferin and Ecotrin.

I read the labels and made my choice,
And then started to walk away.
But before I got far, my eyes became fixed
On some words that froze me to stay.

(continued)

It seemed I had another choice
About the type of pill to swallow.
Gelcaps, geltabs, caplets or tablets
This was getting quite hard to follow.

I knew I should have gone right to the line,
But I wanted to make it just right.
Should it be regular or extra-strength
Or time-release, or P.M. for night.

When a sales clerk asked, "Do you need any
help?"
I said to her, "No thank you ma'am."
But I knew I had another choice to make
On the strength of the milligram.

I knew my wife was counting on me
When I realized my options on size.
Travel, value or economy pack.
The whole store could now hear my cries.

I finally got home to my ailing wife.
Her headache had gotten much worse.
But when we tried to open the bottle
We were doomed with the child-proof curse.

My Corner

As the sun comes up, I'll walk to work.
My office is on the street.
I'll be there in the cold or rain
Or torrid summer heat.

I'll head for the busiest corner
And hope to make it mine.
With luck I'll have a good day
As I raise my homeless sign.

As folks drive by they turn away,
Refuse to meet my eyes.
If only they could read my mind
They'd hear my secret cries.

Some will think this is a scam,
Others just won't care.
But most will drive right by me
As if I wasn't there.

It seems like only yesterday
I had a home and job.
But now what are my options?
Should I beg or should I rob?

Without family or friends
No symphony in sight.
I don't know what is left to do,
Perhaps give up the fight.

(continued)

There's a shelter down the street,
But it's filled and locked up tight.
I look for comfort where I can
And dread the coming night.

Alone on a moldy mattress
I start to sob and pray.
All I need is one to care,
Is this the American way?

Burning Question

It surrounds us where we go by day.
It's with us at work and when we play.

Can't escape at evening or during the night.
Can't be heard or seen as it stays out of sight.

Man or woman, young or old;
It'll grab your soul no matter how bold.

It can cripple our mind or make us weak.
Professional help we may need to seek.

Some days it's hard to get outta bed.
As it gets worse some wish they were dead.

It seems today, it's getting much worse.
What's this abusive and crippling curse?

Maybe it's caused by the way we live.
And the way that we take much more than we give.

Maybe because we demand too much'
Or become too distant and need to touch.

What's caused us to wander and be in this mess?
A destructive force that we call stress.

Wealth

Wealth can surface in various forms.
And it can be different things to different people.
Sometimes it is visible and other times it is hidden.
The importance of wealth may change during our lives.

Wealth can be knowing you've molded the minds of the
young.
Or seeing your children grow up and have children of
their own.
Wealth can be knowing you've made the environment a
safer place
Or giving your life to helping the less fortunate.

Wealth can be camping and hiking the trails of our
national forests
Or devoting your life to seeking cures for disease.
For the architect, it's seeing his art transformed to a
skyscraper
And for some, it's giving yourself to God and teaching his
wisdom.

For others, wealth can be living in a mansion
With fancy cars and expensive clothing.
With people calling you Mr. or Sir,
Where all that matters is success
And the mistreatment of people is power.

But it is these who usually have the least,
And by taking more than giving,
And demanding more than listening,
Have made themselves the poorest of all.

December 10th

This day is special for Karen and I.
Fifty years of bliss you could not buy.

The good, the bad, struggles and smiles.
The kisses and hugs spread out for miles.

The hopes, the dreams we'd both embrace.
The ups, the downs we'd stand and face.

Obstacles yes, but we'd find a way.
Surrender no, together we'd stay.

Argue and fights, but not too much.
Grudges short, with the need to touch.

Setbacks we'd have, but never defeat.
Our love together the special treat.

We're older now, our hearts entwined
We're better now, our love enshrined.

Conclusion

As I reflect back on this book of poetry, I am completely mesmerized at how my mind was able to come up with so many ideas for poems that will penetrate the reader's thought process to reflect on the words that are so real.

How many kids have to die in school shootings before the gun flaws are eliminated. Is the number 1000 a year, 10,000, a million? There has to be a number. What if a politician's child was murdered? Would they then change their mind? But that would then tell everyone that if another child is murdered that's okay as long as it's not theirs. That thinking made for a terrific and impactful poem.

Or the idea that a political party can tell a woman that masks cannot be mandated because it is their own body and then turn around and tell a woman she can't have an abortion and have the woman say, "but it's my body." When written in the form of a poem, the arguments become more compelling.

Or why is it a law that we have to wear a seatbelt, but school buses don't have them even though 1300 children have died from bus accidents? Makes you wonder.

Or why do our police have to confront criminals who have AK-15's when their personal arsenal is a pistol. Are you kidding me?!

Over the years I became very quizzical and started to question our social injustices and the alarming rate of how so many disrupted our lives and the lack of action that was taken to repair them. I added in some humor on some issues like the struggle to wrap leftovers in saran wrap or buying a pair of pants that you would wash in hot water to get them to shrink a half size only to realize that they were pre-shrunk. My mind was always exploring the inadequacies that life throws in our direction or writing some words that would bring us some comical relief.

I'm not sure how my ideas for most of my poems surfaced, but I hope this compilation will challenge the roots of who you have become, and as the sub-title suggests, hopefully make you think, wonder, question and smile!

If anyone would like to comment about these poems, I would love to hear your thoughts. Please email me at: wolf3038@comcast.net.